Manna: Bread Of Life

Manna: Bread Of Life

Devotional and Journal

Shontel Stanford

To order additional copies of this book, contact:
Xlibris Corporation
1-888-795-4274
www.Xlibris.com
Orders@Xlibris.com
60397

Give us this day our daily bread.
Matthew 6:11

Too many Christians are walking around malnourished. It's not like they missed breakfast this morning and they have a little grumbling in their tummy. They're not just hungry. No! That's not it at all! They're dying due to lack of food. Not the natural food we feed our physical bodies but the supernatural food of the spirit that God provides. Just as our physical bodies need food and water to survive and sustain its strength we need to feed our spirits with God's manna to produce spiritual growth and strength.

> *In their hunger you gave them bread from heaven and in their thirst you brought them water from the rock; you told them to go in and take possession of the land you had sworn with uplifted hand to give them. You gave your good Spirit to instruct them. You did not withhold your manna from their mouths, and you gave them water for their thirst.*
> *Nehemiah 9:15, 20*

So what is *Manna?*

1. The food miraculously supplied to the Israelites in the wilderness. Ex. 16:14-36.
2. Any sudden or unexpected Help, advantage, or aid to success.
3. Divine or spiritual food

Most Christians don't have any understanding of what manna really is. Other than the fact that God fed it to the Israelites in the wilderness it holds no value in their lives. However, when I began to study more about manna I learned that it was only good for the day it was given. That meant that the manna from yesterday could not give you any nutritional value today. Why did God make it a point to supply them with new manna every day? I believe that it was so that they would be in expectation every day from their Source, God Almighty. If they had the manna from yesterday they wouldn't need to expect anything from God today. Yet many times we get so busy in our daily routines that we neglect to see God as our only Source all the time. We don't do this on purpose but sometimes things come up that are seemingly more important that staying in His Word every day . . . and well God "understands". Well, God does understand that if we are not in His Word then we cannot hope to live. Yes, we may exist but LIFE is more than just existing day to day. It's about experiencing true joy which is only found in God's presence and by going into His presence joy is manifested in our physical life. It's not something you can obtain by going to church once a week . . . you have to live in His presence!

This is the bread that came down from heaven. Your forefathers ate manna and died, but he who feeds on this bread will live forever.
John 6:58

In the New Testament we read that Jesus is our manna. Therefore, we are to eat of Him every day to survive. John 6:35 says that He is our bread of life and John 10:10 says that He came to give us life more abundantly. Everyone wants the abundant life but in order to obtain that life our conduct should imitate that of Christ and we must be willing to exemplify His life through ours daily. How do we know the conduct of Christ? By dining with Him. Now it's easy to say "I dine with Christ" because you went to the altar and gave Him your life but that's just opening the door. To dine with Him is to eat of Him so that you can grow in the knowledge of His Word. Know this; if you are not producing spiritual growth you're not dining you're dying.

I am the living bread that came down from heaven. If anyone eats of this bread, he will live forever. This bread is my flesh, which I will give for the life of the world."
John 6:51

One of my favorite pieces of art is "You are what you eat" by Edwin Lester. It's a painting of a little boy sitting in the midst of fruit while eating the pages out of his bible. Don't go eat your bible! But what am I saying? Think about this. Our conduct is produced by our character and our character is produced by those things we have learned to believe were right. As children we learned what was acceptable by what we saw (observation), who we were around (association) and what we were taught (teaching). That is our thought system and those thoughts we continue to meditate on produce what we see in our lives and are responsible for the conduct we portray to the world . . . good or bad. John 1:1 tells us that the Word is God then John 1:14 goes on to say the Word became flesh so Jesus Christ is the Word and to eat of Him is to eat the Word. And those who eat the Word become the Word made flesh themselves. You are what you eat! That's how power flows . . . eat the Word until it fills you and then God's power will flow out of you and the enemy will not be able to stop you!

> *Blessed are those who hunger and thirst*
> *for righteousness, for they will be filled.*
> **Matthew 5:6**

When you renew your mind to the Word and Wisdom of God your ways and thoughts will begin to rise up to His level instead of remaining on the level of those who think that they can trust in this world system which is failing thus they are failing along with it. This is why we go to church . . . to get the Word of God to renew our minds! However, we cannot rely on the pastor to feed us only on Sunday morning. We have to feed ourselves all throughout the week. This must be done on purpose in order to know and walk in the will of God for our lives which is the blessing and success!

> *Let the wicked forsake his way and the evil man his thoughts. Let*
> *him turn to the LORD, and he will have mercy on him, and to*
> *our God, for he will freely pardon. "For my thoughts are not your*
> *thoughts, neither are your ways my ways," declares the LORD.*
> **Isaiah 55:7-8**

How do you do this on purpose?

By taking these messages and reflecting on them throughout the day. As you read it aloud you are speaking it into your spirit and giving your mind something to think on all day. The messages are short and simple so that you can take them with you and meditate on them. Each message is derived from a specific scripture and each week there will be one scripture for the entire week to focus on. Since faith comes by hearing and hearing, when you speak the Word you will hear it so that it may be implanted in your heart, just as a seed in good soil, and grow to produce good fruit in your life. Speaking and meditating on the Word will allow you to encourage yourself to give strength in your weakness, joy in your sorrow, understanding in your confusion, and direction when you are lost. It is the Father's desire that you would be refreshed, equipped and empowered through His Word that is implanted in you.

The **Daily Memoir** is your opportunity to write your thoughts or what God may have said to you as you meditated on the Word. Many people say God doesn't speak to them on the contrary God is speaking all the time but we have to align ourselves with His Word so that we can hear clearly. If you've ever tried to speak to someone who spoke a different language you experienced a barrier in your communication . . . that is what it is like when we do not speak God's language. If you truly practice meditating on the Word you will hear from God and whatever He tells you write that. This will help you in building the bridge of communication with God and eventually you will be sure of His voice speaking to you. This will also help you to keep a record of those things that God tells you pertaining to your purpose (who He created you to be and what He created you to do).

"And the LORD answered me, and said, write the vision, and make it plain upon tables, that he may run that readeth it."
Habakkuk 2:2

~S~

But encourage one another daily, as long as it is called today, so that none of you may be hardened by sin's deceitfulness.
Hebrews 3:13

I pray that you be encouraged in heart and that your faith will increase in the revelation of Christ, the Rock of our salvation. It is the Spirit of God that leads you into all truth and He is only able to lead you as much as you allow Him through the Word. As you renew your mind to His holy Word He will manifest Himself to you and through you. Let these words minister to your spirit so that you may be an encouragement to someone else. Do not get weary nor lose focus for as you abide in the Word and wait on God with expectation He will satisfy you. Walk in the blessing!

In Jesus' name, Amen

*Load your plate with a helping of **Manna** and be filled with the **bread of life**!*

DAY 1

Daily Message

The Blessing is in BEING who God called you to BE. Meditate on His Word (Wisdom) until you are confident in who you are!

Daily Manna

[26] God said, Let Us [Father, Son, and Holy Spirit] make mankind in Our image, after Our likeness, and let them have complete authority over the fish of the sea, the birds of the air, the [tame] beasts, and over all of the earth, and over everything that creeps upon the earth.

[27] So God created man in His own image, in the image and likeness of God He created him; male and female He created them.

[28] And God blessed them and said to them, Be fruitful, multiply, and fill the earth, and subdue it [using all its vast resources in the service of God and man]; and have dominion over the fish of the sea, the birds of the air, and over every living creature that moves upon the earth.

Genesis 1:26-28 Amplified Bible (AMP)

Daily Memoir

_____

_____

_____

_____

_____

_____

_____

_____

_____

DAY 2

Daily Message

Embrace that you have been made in God's image (the God-class to have dominion) and walk in His likeness (holy-separated and set apart).

Daily Manna

[26] And God said, Let us make man in our image, after our likeness: and let them have dominion over the fish of the sea, and over the fowl of the air, and over the cattle, and over all the earth, and over every creeping thing that creepeth upon the earth.
[27] So God created man in his own image, in the image of God created he him; male and female created he them.
[28] And God blessed them, and God said unto them, Be fruitful, and multiply, and replenish the earth, and subdue it: and have dominion over the fish of the sea, and over the fowl of the air, and over every living thing that moveth upon the earth.

Genesis 1:26-28 King James Version (KJV)

Daily Memoir

_____

_____

_____

_____

_____

_____

_____

_____

_____

DAY 3

Daily Message

God created us in His image and likeness to glorify Him; for us to recreate ourselves in the world's image brings Him no glory or pleasure.

Daily Manna

[26-28] God spoke: "Let us make human beings in our image, make them reflecting our nature So they can be responsible for the fish in the sea, the birds in the air, the cattle, And, yes, Earth itself, and every animal that moves on the face of Earth."

God created human beings; he created them godlike, Reflecting God's nature. He created them male and female.

God blessed them: "Prosper! Reproduce! Fill Earth! Take charge! Be responsible for fish in the sea and birds in the air, for every living thing that moves on the face of Earth."

Genesis 1:26-28 The Message (MSG)

Daily Memoir

_____
_____
_____
_____
_____
_____
_____
_____
_____
_____
_____

DAY 4

Daily Message

God has given us all dominion and authority in earth, therefore take your rightful stance as an heir and speak in agreement with His word!

Daily Manna

[26] Then God said, "Let Us make man in Our image, according to Our likeness; and let them rule over the fish of the sea and over the birds of the sky and over the cattle and over all the earth, and over every creeping thing that creeps on the earth."

[27] God created man in His own image, in the image of God He created him; male and female He created them.

[28] God blessed them; and God said to them, "Be fruitful and multiply, and fill the earth, and subdue it; and rule over the fish of the sea and over the birds of the sky and over every living thing that moves on the earth."

Genesis 1:26-28 New American Standard Bible (NASB)

Daily Memoir

_____
_____
_____
_____
_____
_____
_____
_____
_____
_____

DAY 5

Daily Message

We have been given ALL authority in Christ (the Word) therefore abide (continue, dwell, remain, stay) in the Word and let His power manifest in you.

Daily Manna

[26] Then God said, "Let us make mankind in our image, in our likeness, so that they may rule over the fish in the sea and the birds in the sky, over the livestock and all the wild animals, and over all the creatures that move along the ground."
[27] So God created mankind in his own image, in the image of God he created them; male and female he created them.
[28] God blessed them and said to them, "Be fruitful and increase in number; fill the earth and subdue it. Rule over the fish in the sea and the birds in the sky and over every living creature that moves on the ground."

Genesis 1:26-28 New International Version (NIV)

Daily Memoir

_____
_____
_____
_____
_____
_____
_____
_____
_____
_____

DAY 6

Daily Message

When God breathed His Spirit in you He filled you with great purpose to be fulfilled as you abide in His word and follow His lead.

Daily Manna

[26] Then God said, "Let Us make man in Our image, according to Our likeness; let them have dominion over the fish of the sea, over the birds of the air, and over the cattle, over all the earth and over every creeping thing that creeps on the earth."
[27] So God created man in His *own* image; in the image of God He created him; male and female He created them.
[28] Then God blessed them, and God said to them, "Be fruitful and multiply; fill the earth and subdue it; have dominion over the fish of the sea, over the birds of the air, and over every living thing that moves on the earth."

Genesis 1:26-28 New King James Version (NKJV)

Daily Memoir

_____
_____
_____
_____
_____
_____
_____
_____
_____

DAY 7

Daily Message

It's God's will that you live in abundance and renew your mind to His Word so you can help others in need. You are blessed (fruitful, multiplying, replenishing, subduing and exercising dominion) TO BE A BLESSING until all the nations of the earth are blessed!

Daily Manna

^{26} Then God said, "Let us make human beings in our image, to be like us. They will reign over the fish in the sea, the birds in the sky, the livestock, all the wild animals on the earth, and the small animals that scurry along the ground."

^{27} So God created human beings in his own image. In the image of God he created them; male and female he created them.

^{28} Then God blessed them and said, "Be fruitful and multiply. Fill the earth and govern it. Reign over the fish in the sea, the birds in the sky, and all the animals that scurry along the ground."

Genesis 1:26-28 New Living Translation (NLT)

Daily Memoir

_____
_____
_____
_____
_____
_____
_____
_____

DAY 8

Daily Message

We believe the Word of God, not our own life experiences, because He fulfills the Promise of His word to those who believe!

Daily Manna

[19] God is not a man, that He should tell or act a lie, neither the son of man, that He should feel repentance or compunction [for what He has promised]. Has He said and shall He not do it? Or has He spoken and shall He not make it good?

Numbers 23:19 Amplified Bible (AMP)

Daily Memoir

_____

_____

_____

_____

_____

_____

_____

_____

_____

_____

_____

_____

_____

_____

DAY 9

Daily Message

We serve the Great God Jehovah. Don't limit His ability to manifest His greatness in you; take the limits off your mind and expect the great!

Daily Manna

[19] God is not a man, that he should lie; neither the son of man, that he should repent: hath he said, and shall he not do it? or hath he spoken, and shall he not make it good?

Numbers 23:19 King James Version (KJV)

Daily Memoir

_____
_____
_____
_____
_____
_____
_____
_____
_____
_____
_____
_____
_____
_____
_____
_____
_____

DAY 10

Daily Message

The Greater One lives in you but He is only able to do (in you) what you are able to believe Him for. When has He ever not kept His promise to you? Just believe!

Daily Manna

God is not man, one given to lies, and not a son of man changing his mind. Does he speak and not do what he says? Does he promise and not come through?

Numbers 23:19 The Message (MSG)

Daily Memoir

_____

_____

_____

_____

_____

_____

_____

_____

_____

_____

_____

_____

_____

_____

_____

DAY 11

Daily Message

If God has EVER done anything for you expect Him to do it again and even greater! He does the seemingly impossible for those who believe!

Daily Manna

[19] "God is not a man, that He should lie, Nor a son of man, that He should repent; Has He said, and will He not do it? Or has He spoken, and will He not make it good?

Numbers 23:19 New American Standard Bible (NASB)

Daily Memoir

_____
_____
_____
_____
_____
_____
_____
_____
_____
_____
_____
_____
_____
_____
_____
_____
_____

DAY 12

Daily Message

God has made the impossible possible for us, who are firmly planted in His Word, so that we may rejoice now in the fulfillment of His promise!

Daily Manna

[19] God is not human, that he should lie, not a human being, that he should change his mind. Does he speak and then not act? Does he promise and not fulfill?

Numbers 23:19 New International Version (NIV)

Daily Memoir

_____
_____
_____
_____
_____
_____
_____
_____
_____
_____
_____
_____
_____
_____
_____
_____

DAY 13

Daily Message

What dream did God put in your heart? Don't let that dream die . . . with God all things are possible!

Daily Manna

[19] "God *is* not a man, that He should lie, Nor a son of man, that He should repent. Has He said, and will He not do? Or has He spoken, and will He not make it good?

Numbers 23:19 New King James Version (NKJV)

Daily Memoir

_____
_____
_____
_____
_____
_____
_____
_____
_____
_____
_____
_____
_____
_____
_____
_____
_____

DAY 14

Daily Message

God doesn't break promises. He has done His part to make sure you have every Promise but if you don't believe Him with your whole heart you won't receive them.

Daily Manna

[19] God is not a man, so he does not lie. He is not human, so he does not change his mind. Has he ever spoken and failed to act? Has he ever promised and not carried it through?

Numbers 23:19 New Living Translation (NLT)

Daily Memoir

_____
_____
_____
_____
_____
_____
_____
_____
_____
_____
_____
_____
_____
_____
_____

DAY 15

Daily Message

Your Outcome is determined by your Income so what are you putting in your spirit? Feed your spirit on God's Word daily and you will be successful.

Daily Manna

[8] This Book of the Law shall not depart out of your mouth, but you shall meditate on it day and night, that you may observe and do according to all that is written in it. For then you shall make your way prosperous, and then you shall deal wisely and have good success.

Joshua 1:8 Amplified Bible (AMP)

Daily Memoir

_____
_____
_____
_____
_____
_____
_____
_____
_____
_____
_____
_____
_____
_____
_____
_____

DAY 16

Daily Message

The Blessing of the Lord is the ability to succeed in whatever we do by abiding in His Word and putting our complete trust in Him! We always win!

Daily Manna

[8] This book of the law shall not depart out of thy mouth; but thou shalt meditate therein day and night, that thou mayest observe to do according to all that is written therein: for then thou shalt make thy way prosperous, and then thou shalt have good success.

Joshua 1:8 King James Version (KJV)

Daily Memoir

_____

_____

_____

_____

_____

_____

_____

_____

_____

_____

_____

_____

_____

_____

_____

DAY 17

Daily Message

You will only go as far as the vision you have; speak the Word until you SEE IT so when you see it you will walk in the path God purposed for you!

Daily Manna

[8] And don't for a minute let this Book of The Revelation be out of mind. Ponder and meditate on it day and night, making sure you practice everything written in it. Then you'll get where you're going; then you'll succeed.

Joshua 1:8 The Message (MSG)

Daily Memoir

_____
_____
_____
_____
_____
_____
_____
_____
_____
_____
_____
_____
_____
_____
_____
_____

DAY 18

Daily Message

Success doesn't come just because you want it; you have to meditate on and speak the Word until you get God's wisdom on your next step to success.

Daily Manna

[8] This book of the law shall not depart from your mouth, but you shall meditate on it day and night, so that you may be careful to do according to all that is written in it; for then you will make your way prosperous, and then you will have success.

Joshua 1:8 New American Standard Bible (NASB)

Daily Memoir

_____

_____

_____

_____

_____

_____

_____

_____

_____

_____

_____

_____

_____

_____

DAY 19

Daily Message

Don't allow distractions to keep you from seeking God's face; for in His Presence are the instructions you need to succeed!

Daily Manna

[8] Keep this Book of the Law always on your lips; meditate on it day and night, so that you may be careful to do everything written in it. Then you will be prosperous and successful.

Joshua 1:8 New International Version (NIV)

Daily Memoir

_____
_____
_____
_____
_____
_____
_____
_____
_____
_____
_____
_____
_____
_____
_____
_____

DAY 20

Daily Message

Those who make light of God's Word set themselves up for failure. It is through abiding in His Wisdom that we walk in victory!

Daily Manna

[8] This Book of the Law shall not depart from your mouth, but you shall meditate in it day and night, that you may observe to do according to all that is written in it. For then you will make your way prosperous, and then you will have good success.

Joshua 1:8 New King James Version (NKJV)

Daily Memoir

_____
_____
_____
_____
_____
_____
_____
_____
_____
_____
_____
_____
_____
_____
_____

DAY 21

Daily Message

The blessing (God's anointing that empowers you to prosper in whatever you do) is released as you make the decision to obey His Word.

Daily Manna

[8] Study this Book of Instruction continually. Meditate on it day and night so you will be sure to obey everything written in it. Only then will you prosper and succeed in all you do.

Joshua 1:8 New Living Translation (NLT)

Daily Memoir

_____

_____

_____

_____

_____

_____

_____

_____

_____

_____

_____

_____

_____

_____

_____

_____

DAY 22

Daily Message

Focus your love on God through obedience to His Word and make Him your desire through worshipping Him then watch Him to do great things on your behalf.

Daily Manna

[9] For the eyes of the Lord run to and fro throughout the whole earth to show Himself strong in behalf of those whose hearts are blameless toward Him. You have done foolishly in this; therefore, from now on you shall have wars.

2 Chronicles 16:9 Amplified Bible (AMP)

Daily Memoir

_____
_____
_____
_____
_____
_____
_____
_____
_____
_____
_____
_____
_____
_____

DAY 23

Daily Message

The human spirit is so big it can only be filled by God, Himself and when we allow Him to fill us He will add to us our heart's desires. He is the MORE THAN ENOUGH GOD!

Daily Manna

⁹ For the eyes of the LORD run to and fro throughout the whole earth, to shew himself strong in the behalf of them whose heart is perfect toward him. Herein thou hast done foolishly: therefore from henceforth thou shalt have wars.

2 Chronicles 16:9 King James Version (KJV)

Daily Memoir

_____
_____
_____
_____
_____
_____
_____
_____
_____
_____
_____
_____
_____
_____

DAY 24

Daily Message

In all things walk in Love, for God is love and if we continue to walk in Him the power of God will abide in us and NOTHING WILL BE IMPOSSIBLE!

Daily Manna

[9] GOD is always on the alert, constantly on the lookout for people who are totally committed to him. You were foolish to go for human help when you could have had God's help. Now you're in trouble—one round of war after another.

2 Chronicles 16:9 The Message (MSG)

Daily Memoir

_____
_____
_____
_____
_____
_____
_____
_____
_____
_____
_____
_____
_____
_____
_____
_____

DAY 25

Daily Message

Without the Word of God we are not capable of rendering our heart completely to God. Meditate on the Word until He is your desire.

Daily Manna

⁹ For the eyes of the LORD move to and fro throughout the earth that He may strongly support those whose heart is completely His. You have acted foolishly in this. Indeed, from now on you will surely have wars."

2 Chronicles 16:9 New American Standard Bible (NASB)

Daily Memoir

_____
_____
_____
_____
_____
_____
_____
_____
_____
_____
_____
_____
_____
_____
_____
_____
_____

DAY 26

Daily Message

The Word is of no use to you unless it is implanted in your heart. Therefore by implanting the Word (acting on it) you will release the power of the Word in your life.

Daily Manna

[9] For the eyes of the LORD range throughout the earth to strengthen those whose hearts are fully committed to him. You have done a foolish thing, and from now on you will be at war."

2 Chronicles 16:9 New International Version (NIV)

Daily Memoir

_____

_____

_____

_____

_____

_____

_____

_____

_____

_____

_____

_____

_____

_____

_____

_____

DAY 27

Daily Message

Christ came to separate us from the world for His purpose. Abide in His word until it He is made strong in you to fulfill His purpose in Earth.

Daily Manna

[9] For the eyes of the LORD run to and fro throughout the whole earth, to show Himself strong on behalf of *those* whose heart *is* loyal to Him. In this you have done foolishly; therefore from now on you shall have wars."

2 Chronicles 16:9 New King James Version (NKJV)

Daily Memoir

_____
_____
_____
_____
_____
_____
_____
_____
_____
_____
_____
_____
_____
_____
_____
_____
_____

DAY 28

Daily Message

We don't receive the promises of God because we want them; we receive them because we abide, continue, dwell, remain and stay in Him (the Word) and refuse to be moved.

Daily Manna

[9] The eyes of the LORD search the whole earth in order to strengthen those whose hearts are fully committed to him. What a fool you have been! From now on you will be at war.

2 Chronicles 16:9 New Living Translation (NLT)

Daily Memoir

_____
_____
_____
_____
_____
_____
_____
_____
_____
_____
_____
_____
_____
_____

DAY 29

Daily Message

Your praise ushers in God's power in your situation! Don't complain about what you're facing; start praising and watch God fight for you!

Daily Manna

[22] And when they began to sing and to praise, the Lord set ambushments against the men of Ammon, Moab, and Mount Seir who had come against Judah, and they were [self-] slaughtered;

2 Chronicles 20:22 Amplified Bible (AMP)

Daily Memoir

_____
_____
_____
_____
_____
_____
_____
_____
_____
_____
_____
_____
_____
_____
_____
_____

DAY 30

Daily Message

Joy is the unstoppable spiritual force that gives you strength to accomplish all things and be victorious. Get God's joy today!

Daily Manna

[22] And when they began to sing and to praise, the LORD set ambushments against the children of Ammon, Moab, and mount Seir, which were come against Judah; and they were smitten.

2 Chronicles 20:22 King James Version (KJV)

Daily Memoir

_____
_____
_____
_____
_____
_____
_____
_____
_____
_____
_____
_____
_____
_____
_____
_____
_____
_____

DAY 31

Daily Message

It's the joy of the Lord that is your strength but if you never get in His presence you will not receive His joy therefore you will lack the strength you need to praise into your victorious place.

Daily Manna

[22] As soon as they started shouting and praising, GOD set ambushes against the men of Ammon, Moab, and Mount Seir as they were attacking Judah, and they all ended up dead.

2 Chronicles 20:22 The Message (MSG)

Daily Memoir

_____
_____
_____
_____
_____
_____
_____
_____
_____
_____
_____
_____
_____
_____
_____
_____
_____

DAY 32

Daily Message

God is always with us but it's our responsibility to fellowship with Him daily . . . that's how we get the strength to endure the day!

Daily Manna

[22] When they began singing and praising, the LORD set ambushes against the sons of Ammon, Moab and Mount Seir, who had come against Judah; so they were routed.

2 Chronicles 20:22 New American Standard Bible (NASB)

Daily Memoir

_____

_____

_____

_____

_____

_____

_____

_____

_____

_____

_____

_____

_____

_____

DAY 33

Daily Message

There is nothing like dwelling in God's Presence. Don't seek to be in His Presence for things but to praise Him in all His greatness!

Daily Manna

²² As they began to sing and praise, the LORD set ambushes against the men of Ammon and Moab and Mount Seir who were invading Judah, and they were defeated.

2 Chronicles 20:22 New International Version (NIV)

Daily Memoir

_____
_____
_____
_____
_____
_____
_____
_____
_____
_____
_____
_____
_____
_____
_____
_____

DAY 34

Daily Message

In the midst of whatever you are facing God will give you His perfect peace so that you can walk right through it with triumphant praise! Glory!

Daily Manna

22 Now when they began to sing and to praise, the LORD set ambushes against the people of Ammon, Moab, and Mount Seir, who had come against Judah; and they were defeated.

2 Chronicles 20:22 New King James Version (NKJV)

Daily Memoir

_____
_____
_____
_____
_____
_____
_____
_____
_____
_____
_____
_____
_____
_____
_____
_____
_____
_____

DAY 35

Daily Message

Discouragement comes from putting your focus on your current situation instead of God, Who always leads you in triumphant victory!

Daily Manna

²² At the very moment they began to sing and give praise, the LORD caused the armies of Ammon, Moab, and Mount Seir to start fighting among themselves.

2 Chronicles 20:22 New Living Translation (NLT)

Daily Memoir

DAY 36

Daily Message

You will believe whatever/whoever you surround yourself with and your words will manifest what you believe . . . negative or positive.

Daily Manna

¹ BLESSED (HAPPY, fortunate, prosperous, and enviable) is the man who walks and lives not in the counsel of the ungodly [following their advice, their plans and purposes], nor stands [submissive and inactive] in the path where sinners walk, nor sits down [to relax and rest] where the scornful [and the mockers] gather.
² But his delight and desire are in the law of the Lord, and on His law (the precepts, the instructions, the teachings of God) he habitually meditates (ponders and studies) by day and by night.
³ And he shall be like a tree firmly planted [and tended] by the streams of water, ready to bring forth its fruit in its season; its leaf also shall not fade or wither; and everything he does shall prosper [and come to maturity].

Psalm 1:1-3 Amplified Bible (AMP)

Daily Memoir

_____
_____
_____
_____
_____
_____
_____
_____

DAY 37

Daily Message

We are human beings not human doings; first embrace who God has called you to BE then you will flourish in all that He has told you to DO.

Daily Manna

[1] Blessed is the man that walketh not in the counsel of the ungodly, nor standeth in the way of sinners, nor sitteth in the seat of the scornful.

[2] But his delight is in the law of the LORD; and in his law doth he meditate day and night.

[3] And he shall be like a tree planted by the rivers of water, that bringeth forth his fruit in his season; his leaf also shall not wither; and whatsoever he doeth shall prosper.

Psalm 1:1-3 King James Version (KJV)

Daily Memoir

_____
_____
_____
_____
_____
_____
_____
_____
_____
_____
_____
_____

DAY 38

Daily Message

Don't let other people's progress frustrate your faith. As long as you remain rooted in the Word you will bring forth your fruit in your season.

Daily Manna

[1] How well God must like you—you don't hang out at Sin Saloon, you don't slink along Dead-End Road, you don't go to Smart-Mouth College.

[2-3] Instead you thrill to GOD's Word, you chew on Scripture day and night. You're a tree replanted in Eden, bearing fresh fruit every month, Never dropping a leaf, always in blossom.

Psalm 1:1-3 The Message (MSG)

Daily Memoir

_____
_____
_____
_____
_____
_____
_____
_____
_____
_____
_____
_____
_____
_____
_____
_____

DAY 39

Daily Message

God is only limited (in your life) to what you will believe Him for. Raise your level of expectation to His Word by meditating in it day and night.

Daily Manna

[1] How blessed is the man who does not walk in the counsel of the wicked, Nor stand in the path of sinners, Nor sit in the seat of scoffers!
[2] But his delight is in the law of the LORD, And in His law he meditates day and night.
[3] He will be like a tree *firmly* planted by streams of water, Which yields its fruit in its season And its leaf does not wither; And in whatever he does, he prospers.

Psalm 1:1-3 New American Standard Bible (NASB)

Daily Memoir

_____
_____
_____
_____
_____
_____
_____
_____
_____
_____
_____
_____

DAY 40

Daily Message

You have to let go of some people so you can see the vision God has for your life and get His wisdom to walk it out!

Daily Manna

¹ Blessed is the one who does not walk in step with the wicked or stand in the way that sinners take or sit in the company of mockers,

² but whose delight is in the law of the LORD, and who meditates on his law day and night.

³ That person is like a tree planted by streams of water, which yields its fruit in season and whose leaf does not wither—whatever they do prospers.

Psalm 1:1-3 New International Version (NIV)

Daily Memoir

_____

_____

_____

_____

_____

_____

_____

_____

_____

_____

_____

_____

_____

DAY 41

Daily Message

You are going to have to separate from a lot of people before you will see the vision God has spoken to you and accomplish that purpose in your life.

Daily Manna

[1] Blessed *is* the man Who walks not in the counsel of the ungodly, Nor stands in the path of sinners, Nor sits in the seat of the scornful;
[2] But his delight is in the law of the LORD, And in His law he meditates day and night.
[3] He shall be like a tree Planted by the rivers of water, That brings forth its fruit in its season, Whose leaf also shall not wither; And whatever he does shall prosper.

Psalm 1:1-3 New King James Version (NKJV)

Daily Memoir

DAY 42

Daily Message

We will never accomplish what we cannot see ourselves doing. Focus on the vision God has put in your heart until its real to you.

Daily Manna

¹ Oh, the joys of those who do not follow the advice of the wicked, or stand around with sinners, or join in with mockers.
² But they delight in the law of the LORD, meditating on it day and night.
³ They are like trees planted along the riverbank, bearing fruit each season. Their leaves never wither, and they prosper in all they do.

Psalm 1:1-3 New Living Translation (NLT)

Daily Memoir

_____
_____
_____
_____
_____
_____
_____
_____
_____
_____
_____
_____
_____
_____

DAY 43

Daily Message

When you make being in the Presence of God your priority He will pour out His wisdom and power on you. In His Presence is where you are strongest!

Daily Manna

[11] You will show me the path of life; in Your presence is fullness of joy, at Your right hand there are pleasures forevermore.

Psalm 16:11 Amplified Bible (AMP)

Daily Memoir

_____
_____
_____
_____
_____
_____
_____
_____
_____
_____
_____
_____
_____
_____
_____
_____

DAY 44

Daily Message

God is the source of all joy! Instead of relying on people or things to provide you with happiness seek to be in the Presence of the Lord God!

Daily Manna

[11] Thou wilt shew me the path of life: in thy presence is fullness of joy; at thy right hand there are pleasures for evermore.

Psalm 16:11 King James Version (KJV)

Daily Memoir

_____
_____
_____
_____
_____
_____
_____
_____
_____
_____
_____
_____
_____
_____
_____
_____
_____
_____

DAY 45

Daily Message

When you spend time in God's Presence there is fullness of joy so you can go back and laugh in the face of the enemy. SMILE! YOU WIN!

Daily Manna

[11] Now you've got my feet on the life path, all radiant from the shining of your face. Ever since you took my hand, I'm on the right way.

Psalm 16:11 The Message (MSG)

Daily Memoir

_____
_____
_____
_____
_____
_____
_____
_____
_____
_____
_____
_____
_____
_____
_____
_____
_____
_____

DAY 46

Daily Message

Joy is the results of spending time in God's Presence and by His joy we are empowered with strength to overcome anything.

Daily Manna

[11] You will make known to me the path of life; In Your presence is fullness of joy; In Your right hand there are pleasures forever.

Psalm 16:11 New American Standard Bible (NASB)

Daily Memoir

_____
_____
_____
_____
_____
_____
_____
_____
_____
_____
_____
_____
_____
_____
_____
_____

DAY 47

Daily Message

This is the day the Lord has made and it is He who has given us this abundant life to enjoy, for it is in Him that we possess the fullness of joy!

Daily Manna

[11] You make known to me the path of life; you will fill me with joy in your presence, with eternal pleasures at your right hand.

Psalm 16:11 New International Version (NIV)

Daily Memoir

_____
_____
_____
_____
_____
_____
_____
_____
_____
_____
_____
_____
_____
_____
_____
_____
_____
_____

DAY 48

Daily Message

Joy is the spiritual force God has given to us to overcome all things but we have to get in His presence to receive it.

Daily Manna

[11] You will show me the path of life; In Your presence *is* fullness of joy; At Your right hand *are* pleasures forevermore.

Psalm 16:11 New King James Version (NKJV)

Daily Memoir

_____
_____
_____
_____
_____
_____
_____
_____
_____
_____
_____
_____
_____
_____
_____
_____
_____

DAY 49

Daily Message

It is impossible to be sad in the presence of God when in His presence is the fullness of joy. Get your mind off of you and get full on Him!

Daily Manna

[11] You will show me the way of life, granting me the joy of your presence and the pleasures of living with you forever.

Psalm 16:11 New Living Translation (NLT)

Daily Memoir

_____
_____
_____
_____
_____
_____
_____
_____
_____
_____
_____
_____
_____
_____
_____
_____
_____

DAY 50

Daily Message

Praying in the spirit allows God to shine His Revelation light in you so that you know what to do and when to do it.

Daily Manna

[23] If you will turn (repent) and give heed to my reproof, behold, I [Wisdom] will pour out my spirit upon you, I will make my words known to you.

Proverbs 1:23 Amplified Bible (AMP)

Daily Memoir

_____
_____
_____
_____
_____
_____
_____
_____
_____
_____
_____
_____
_____
_____
_____
_____
_____
_____

DAY 51

Daily Message

God has an answer for everything you face; dig into His Word to find it then meditate on it until He gives you revelation for your situation.

Daily Manna

[23] Turn you at my reproof: behold, I will pour out my spirit unto you, I will make known my words unto you.

Proverbs 1:23 King James Version (KJV)

Daily Memoir

_____
_____
_____
_____
_____
_____
_____
_____
_____
_____
_____
_____
_____
_____
_____
_____
_____
_____

DAY 52

Daily Message

God has never forgotten you; He is always there speaking and telling you what to do next but you have to make yourself available to hear from Him.

Daily Manna

[23] About face! I can revise your life. Look, I'm ready to pour out my spirit on you; I'm ready to tell you all I know.

Proverbs 1:23 The Message (MSG)

Daily Memoir

_____

_____

_____

_____

_____

_____

_____

_____

_____

_____

_____

_____

_____

_____

_____

_____

DAY 53

Daily Message

Revelation of God's Word will cause you to impact the world if you don't let the world impact your belief of God's Word first.

Daily Manna

[23] "Turn to my reproof, Behold, I will pour out my spirit on you; I will make my words known to you.

Proverbs 1:23 New American Standard Bible (NASB)

Daily Memoir

DAY 54

Daily Message

God doesn't work in *mysterious* ways He works according to His Word and it is revealed to us as we take the time to study it.

Daily Manna

[23] Repent at my rebuke! Then I will pour out my thoughts to you, I will make known to you my teachings.

Proverbs 1:23 New International Version (NIV)

Daily Memoir

_____

_____

_____

_____

_____

_____

_____

_____

_____

_____

_____

_____

_____

_____

_____

_____

_____

DAY 55

Daily Message

It's the revelation of God's word that ushers in the Blessing! You don't have to wait until New Year's day to make a resolution. Make the shift NOW!

Daily Manna

²³ Turn at my rebuke; Surely I will pour out my spirit on you; I will make my words known to you.

Proverbs 1:23 New King James Version (NKJV)

Daily Memoir

_____
_____
_____
_____
_____
_____
_____
_____
_____
_____
_____
_____
_____
_____
_____
_____
_____
_____

DAY 56

Daily Message

It is the revelation of God's word that brings light to your life so you don't have to stay in the same situation.

(My prayer for you is that God would direct you to your assigned pastor so you can be fed on knowledge and understanding so that God can give you revelation.)

Daily Manna

[23] Come and listen to my counsel. I'll share my heart with you and make you wise.

Proverbs 1:23 New Living Translation (NLT)

Daily Memoir

_____
_____
_____
_____
_____
_____
_____
_____
_____
_____
_____
_____
_____
_____

DAY 57

Daily Message

God's Word is the standard to which we live our lives! We are only right when our words, thoughts and behavior line up with His Word!

Daily Manna

[5] Lean on, trust in, and be confident in the Lord with all your heart and mind and do not rely on your own insight or understanding.

[6] In all your ways know, recognize, and acknowledge Him, and He will direct and make straight and plain your paths.

Proverbs 3:5-6 Amplified Bible (AMP)

Daily Memoir

_____
_____
_____
_____
_____
_____
_____
_____
_____
_____
_____
_____
_____
_____
_____
_____

DAY 58

Daily Message

Wisdom not only tells you how to but should you do something and when to do it. Seek God for wisdom so that you are on the sweat less path.

Daily Manna

⁵ Trust in the LORD with all thine heart; and lean not unto thine own understanding.
⁶ In all thy ways acknowledge him, and he shall direct thy paths.

Proverbs 3:5-6 King James Version (KJV)

Daily Memoir

_____
_____
_____
_____
_____
_____
_____
_____
_____
_____
_____
_____
_____
_____
_____
_____
_____

DAY 59

Daily Message

Unless we give God all of us we are not fully trusting in Him. Trust requires that we are not looking to a plan B.

Daily Manna

[5] Trust God from the bottom of your heart; don't try to figure out everything on your own.

[6] Listen for God's voice in everything you do, everywhere you go; he's the one who will keep you on track.

Proverbs 3:5-6 The Message (MSG)

Daily Memoir

_____
_____
_____
_____
_____
_____
_____
_____
_____
_____
_____
_____
_____
_____
_____
_____

DAY 60

Daily Message

Without full reliance on God's Word we cannot walk in the wisdom needed to fulfill our purpose. God's plan is perfect . . . trust Him!

Daily Manna

⁵ Trust in the LORD with all your heart And do not lean on your own understanding.
⁶ In all your ways acknowledge Him, And He will make your paths straight.

Proverbs 3:5-6 New American Standard Bible (NASB)

Daily Memoir

_____
_____
_____
_____
_____
_____
_____
_____
_____
_____
_____
_____
_____
_____
_____

DAY 61

Daily Message

A wise person seeks God for the direction of his/her life instead of relying on their own past experiences and worldly wisdom.

Daily Manna

[5] Trust in the LORD with all your heart and lean not on your own understanding;

[6] in all your ways submit to him, and he will make your paths straight

Proverbs 3:5-6 New International Version (NIV)

Daily Memoir

_____
_____
_____
_____
_____
_____
_____
_____
_____
_____
_____
_____
_____
_____
_____
_____
_____

DAY 62

Daily Message

God is faithful to direct your path when you fully trust in Him; when you're led by God you can't get lost or end up at the wrong place! Glory to God!

Daily Manna

[5] Trust in the LORD with all your heart, And lean not on your own understanding;

[6] In all your ways acknowledge Him, And He shall direct your paths.

Proverbs 3:5-6 New King James Version (NKJV)

Daily Memoir

_____
_____
_____
_____
_____
_____
_____
_____
_____
_____
_____
_____
_____
_____
_____
_____

DAY 63

Daily Message

In order to accomplish the great things God has created you for you must completely trust in Him and rely on His wisdom to direct you!

Daily Manna

[5] Trust in the LORD with all your heart; do not depend on your own understanding.
[6] Seek his will in all you do, and he will show you which path to take.

Proverbs 3:5-6 New Living Translation (NLT)

Daily Memoir

_____
_____
_____
_____
_____
_____
_____
_____
_____
_____
_____
_____
_____
_____
_____
_____
_____

DAY 64

Daily Message

The pursuit of happiness leaves you unfulfilled but the pursuit of Godly wisdom fulfills all your needs! Get Wisdom!

Daily Manna

[13] Happy (blessed, fortunate, enviable) is the man who finds skillful and godly Wisdom, and the man who gets understanding [drawing it forth from God's Word and life's experiences],

Proverbs 3:13 Amplified Bible (AMP)

Daily Memoir

_____
_____
_____
_____
_____
_____
_____
_____
_____
_____
_____
_____
_____
_____
_____
_____

DAY 65

Daily Message

If you find little value in God's Word (which is Wisdom) you will never walk out the destiny He has for you which leads to happiness.

Daily Manna

[13] Happy is the man that findeth wisdom, and the man that getteth understanding.

Proverbs 3:13 King James Version (KJV)

Daily Memoir

_____
_____
_____
_____
_____
_____
_____
_____
_____
_____
_____
_____
_____
_____
_____
_____
_____
_____

DAY 66

Daily Message

Seeking the Wisdom of God adds success, health and prosperity. Those who are led by Wisdom are happy. Get your mind on seeking WISDOM!

Daily Manna

[13] You're blessed when you meet Lady Wisdom, when you make friends with Madame Insight.

Proverbs 3:13 The Message (MSG)

Daily Memoir

_____

_____

_____

_____

_____

_____

_____

_____

_____

_____

_____

_____

_____

_____

_____

_____

_____

DAY 67

Daily Message

Happiness is a result of finding God's Wisdom. There is no happiness outside of God's Word because He has the perfect plan for your life.

Daily Manna

[13] How blessed is the man who finds wisdom And the man who gains understanding.

Proverbs 3:13 New American Standard Bible (NASB)

Daily Memoir

_____
_____
_____
_____
_____
_____
_____
_____
_____
_____
_____
_____
_____
_____
_____
_____
_____
_____

DAY 68

Daily Message

Chasing after things will never fill your heart but when you make Wisdom your primary pursuit you will be blessed (happy) and those things will be added.

Daily Manna

[13] Blessed are those who find wisdom, those who gain understanding,

Proverbs 3:13 New International Version (NIV)

Daily Memoir

_____
_____
_____
_____
_____
_____
_____
_____
_____
_____
_____
_____
_____
_____
_____
_____
_____
_____

DAY 69

Daily Message

Happiness is a product of walking in the Wisdom of God because the direction He leads you in is where your blessings are.

Daily Manna

[13] Happy *is* the man *who* finds wisdom, And the man *who* gains understanding;

Proverbs 3:13 New King James Version (NKJV)

Daily Memoir

_____
_____
_____
_____
_____
_____
_____
_____
_____
_____
_____
_____
_____
_____
_____
_____
_____
_____

DAY 70

Daily Message

Happiness is a choice! Make the choice to seek the wisdom of God so that you may dwell in His Presence to be full of His joy and peace!

Daily Manna

[13] Joyful is the person who finds wisdom, the one who gains understanding.

Proverbs 3:13 New Living Translation (NLT)

Daily Memoir

_____
_____
_____
_____
_____
_____
_____
_____
_____
_____
_____
_____
_____
_____
_____
_____

DAY 71

Daily Message

God gives wisdom freely to those who pursue His wisdom as the most important thing in their life. Make wisdom your pursuit!

Daily Manna

[7] The beginning of Wisdom is: get Wisdom (skillful and godly Wisdom)! [For skillful and godly Wisdom is the principal thing.] And with all you have gotten, get understanding (discernment, comprehension, and interpretation).

Proverbs 4:7 Amplified Bible (AMP)

Daily Memoir

_____
_____
_____
_____
_____
_____
_____
_____
_____
_____
_____
_____
_____
_____
_____
_____

DAY 72

Daily Message

If you're not seeking the wisdom of God anything else you're seeking is a waste of time.

Daily Manna

[7] Wisdom is the principal thing; therefore get wisdom: and with all thy getting get understanding.

Proverbs 4:7 King James Version (KJV)

Daily Memoir

_____
_____
_____
_____
_____
_____
_____
_____
_____
_____
_____
_____
_____
_____
_____
_____
_____

DAY 73

Daily Message

Nothing is more important than God's Word. Live a life that says 'Christ is my life and everything else is an added benefit'.

Daily Manna

[7] Above all and before all, do this: Get Wisdom! Write this at the top of your list: Get Understanding!

Proverbs 4:7 The Message (MSG)

Daily Memoir

_____

_____

_____

_____

_____

_____

_____

_____

_____

_____

_____

_____

_____

_____

_____

_____

_____

DAY 74

Daily Message

The wisdom of God is not gained by simply wanting it; we must seek it with all of our heart as the primary pursuit of our happiness!

Daily Manna

[7] "The beginning of wisdom *is*: Acquire wisdom; And with all your acquiring, get understanding.

Proverbs 4:7 New American Standard Bible (NASB)

Daily Memoir

_____
_____
_____
_____
_____
_____
_____
_____
_____
_____
_____
_____
_____
_____
_____
_____
_____
_____

DAY 75

Daily Message

God gives us sweat less victory when we put forth effort and time to get the wisdom needed to win!

Daily Manna

[7] The beginning of wisdom is this: Get wisdom. Though it cost all you have, get understanding.

Proverbs 4:7 New International Version (NIV)

Daily Memoir

_____

_____

_____

_____

_____

_____

_____

_____

_____

_____

_____

_____

_____

_____

_____

_____

_____

DAY 76

Daily Message

You can't get God's wisdom without investing your whole heart! Wisdom must be your hearts' desire to receive the blessings God has for you!

Daily Manna

[7] Wisdom *is* the principal thing; *Therefore* get wisdom. And in all your getting, get understanding.

Proverbs 4:7 New King James Version (NKJV)

Daily Memoir

_____
_____
_____
_____
_____
_____
_____
_____
_____
_____
_____
_____
_____
_____
_____
_____
_____

DAY 77

Daily Message

Wisdom is the most important thing we can ask of God and in getting it we will be led into the path He predestined for us and walk in the blessing!

Daily Manna

[7] Getting wisdom is the wisest thing you can do! And whatever else you do, develop good judgment.

Proverbs 4:7 New Living Translation (NLT)

Daily Memoir

_____

_____

_____

_____

_____

_____

_____

_____

_____

_____

_____

_____

_____

_____

_____

_____

DAY 78

Daily Message

The good life is found on the path Wisdom has chosen for you; there is no success without abiding in the Wisdom of God to guide your steps.

Daily Manna

[18] Riches and honor are with me, enduring wealth and righteousness (uprightness in every area and relation, and right standing with God).

Proverbs 8:18 Amplified Bible (AMP)

Daily Memoir

_____
_____
_____
_____
_____
_____
_____
_____
_____
_____
_____
_____
_____
_____
_____
_____
_____
_____

DAY 79

Daily Message

If your focus is to 'get rich or die trying' you may get rich but it will be the death of you! Get Wisdom to live long with great wealth—beats the alternative!

Daily Manna

[18] Riches and honour are with me; yea, durable riches and righteousness.

Proverbs 8:18 King James Version (KJV)

Daily Memoir

_____

_____

_____

_____

_____

_____

_____

_____

_____

_____

_____

_____

_____

_____

_____

_____

_____

_____

DAY 80

Daily Message

If you don't know your purpose you will fill your life with things to feel valued, but when you seek God's Wisdom for your purpose you will never be without value.

Daily Manna

Wealth and Glory accompany me—also substantial Honor and a Good Name.

Proverbs 8:18 The Message (MSG)

Daily Memoir

_____

_____

_____

_____

_____

_____

_____

_____

_____

_____

_____

_____

_____

_____

_____

_____

DAY 81

Daily Message

We can't see the manifestation of God's plan in our lives until we grab hold of His wisdom; with wisdom on our side life is good!

Daily Manna

[18] "Riches and honor are with me, Enduring wealth and righteousness.

Proverbs 8:18 New American Standard Bible (NASB)

Daily Memoir

_____
_____
_____
_____
_____
_____
_____
_____
_____
_____
_____
_____
_____
_____
_____
_____
_____
_____
_____

DAY 82

Daily Message

The pursuit of God's Wisdom brings eternal prosperity . . . spirit, soul, body, socially and FINANCIALLY.

Daily Manna

[18] With me are riches and honor, enduring wealth and prosperity.

Proverbs 8:18 New International Version (NIV)

Daily Memoir

_____
_____
_____
_____
_____
_____
_____
_____
_____
_____
_____
_____
_____
_____
_____
_____
_____
_____

DAY 83

Daily Message

The Blessing is not a "thing"; it is God's anointing that empowers you to prosper in all that you do for the building up of God's Kingdom!

Daily Manna

[18] Riches and honor *are* with me, Enduring riches and righteousness.

Proverbs 8:18 New King James Version (NKJV)

Daily Memoir

_____
_____
_____
_____
_____
_____
_____
_____
_____
_____
_____
_____
_____
_____
_____
_____
_____
_____

DAY 84

Daily Message

God created me to be rich and it makes Him happy for me to walk in it . . . I just choose to let Him have His way because I'm a God pleaser!

Daily Manna

[18] I have riches and honor, as well as enduring wealth and justice.

Proverbs 8:18 New Living Translation (NLT)

Daily Memoir

_____
_____
_____
_____
_____
_____
_____
_____
_____
_____
_____
_____
_____
_____
_____
_____
_____
_____
_____

DAY 85

Daily Message

Wisdom should lead our hearts' desire so that through committing our lives to Him and taking the path He predestined we fulfill His purpose.

Daily Manna

[9] A man's mind plans his way, but the Lord directs his steps and makes them sure.

Proverbs 16:9 Amplified Bible (AMP)

Daily Memoir

_____
_____
_____
_____
_____
_____
_____
_____
_____
_____
_____
_____
_____
_____
_____
_____
_____
_____

DAY 86

Daily Message

We were designed to do the impossible; we will accomplish that when we ABIDE in Christ to allow Him to direct us in the way He desires.

Daily Manna

[9] A man's heart deviseth his way: but the LORD directeth his steps.

Proverbs 16:9 King James Version (KJV)

Daily Memoir

_____
_____
_____
_____
_____
_____
_____
_____
_____
_____
_____
_____
_____
_____
_____
_____
_____
_____
_____
_____

DAY 87

Daily Message

When we acknowledge God in everything we do, giving His plan priority in our everyday lives our steps will not be hindered.

Daily Manna

[9] We plan the way we want to live, but only GOD makes us able to live it.

Proverbs 16:9 The Message (MSG)

Daily Memoir

_____
_____
_____
_____
_____
_____
_____
_____
_____
_____
_____
_____
_____
_____
_____
_____
_____
_____
_____

DAY 88

Daily Message

We all have a God-given purpose but it's only when we are willing to walk the path He has chosen we will find success.

Daily Manna

[9] The mind of man plans his way, But the LORD directs his steps.

Proverbs 16:9 New American Standard Bible (NASB)

Daily Memoir

_____
_____
_____
_____
_____
_____
_____
_____
_____
_____
_____
_____
_____
_____
_____
_____
_____

DAY 89

Daily Message

God has already predestined the path to the good life for us now we just have to tune in to what He is saying and completely trust Him.

Daily Manna

[9] In their hearts humans plan their course, but the LORD establishes their steps.

Proverbs 16:9 New International Version (NIV)

Daily Memoir

_____
_____
_____
_____
_____
_____
_____
_____
_____
_____
_____
_____
_____
_____
_____
_____
_____
_____

DAY 90

Daily Message

God's best is on the other side of your unqualified/unconditional YES. He can't do what you ask until you are WILLING to do what He asks of you FIRST.

Daily Manna

⁹ A man's heart plans his way, But the LORD directs his steps.

Proverbs 16:9 New King James Version (NKJV)

Daily Memoir

_____
_____
_____
_____
_____
_____
_____
_____
_____
_____
_____
_____
_____
_____
_____
_____
_____
_____

DAY 91

Daily Message

Saying YES to God's will is the qualifier to receiving God's best for your life! Don't allow "your plans" to stop you from walking in your destiny.

Daily Manna

[9] We can make our plans, but the LORD determines our steps.

Proverbs 16:9 New Living Translation (NLT)

Daily Memoir

_____

_____

_____

_____

_____

_____

_____

_____

_____

_____

_____

_____

_____

_____

_____

_____

_____

_____

DAY 92

Daily Message

Your life is altered by what you speak and believe. Change the way you think by renewing your mind to the Word of God and you will change your life.

Daily Manna

[7] For as he thinks in his heart, so is he.

Proverbs 23:7 Amplified Bible (AMP)

Daily Memoir

_____
_____
_____
_____
_____
_____
_____
_____
_____
_____
_____
_____
_____
_____
_____
_____
_____

DAY 93

Daily Message

You are what you think. Don't allow thoughts contrary to God's Word to settle in your mind. Open your mouth and speak what His Word says about you!

Daily Manna

[7] For as he thinketh in his heart, so is he

Proverbs 23:7 King James Version (KJV)

Daily Memoir

_____
_____
_____
_____
_____
_____
_____
_____
_____
_____
_____
_____
_____
_____
_____
_____
_____
_____

DAY 94

Daily Message

You can't have a loser mentality and Win! You can't have a sickness mentality and be well! You can't have a poverty mentality and be rich!

Daily Manna

[7] What he thinks is what he really is.

Proverbs 23:7 Good News Translation (GNT)

Daily Memoir

_____
_____
_____
_____
_____
_____
_____
_____
_____
_____
_____
_____
_____
_____
_____
_____
_____
_____

DAY 95

Daily Message

You will only do what you can see yourself doing. Renew your mind to the vision God has for you and expect great things.

Daily Manna

[7] For as he thinks within himself, so he is.

Proverbs 23:7 New American Standard Bible (NASB)

Daily Memoir

_____
_____
_____
_____
_____
_____
_____
_____
_____
_____
_____
_____
_____
_____
_____
_____
_____
_____

DAY 96

Daily Message

God requires you to change the way you think to receive His best for your life! Renew your mind by meditating on what the Word says about you!

Daily Manna

⁷ For as he hath thought in his soul, so [is] he

Proverbs 23:7 Young's Literal Translation (YLT)

Daily Memoir

_____
_____
_____
_____
_____
_____
_____
_____
_____
_____
_____
_____
_____
_____
_____
_____
_____
_____

DAY 97

Daily Message

You can't renew your mind (change the way you think) without opening your mouth. Speak the Word until you believe the Word so you can speak it and receive it!

Daily Manna

[7] For as he thinks in his heart, so *is* he.

Proverbs 23:7 New King James Version (NKJV)

Daily Memoir

_____

_____

_____

_____

_____

_____

_____

_____

_____

_____

_____

_____

_____

_____

_____

_____

_____

DAY 98

Daily Message

We are limited by our own thinking. As we meditate on the Word our minds will be renewed and we will begin to believe the impossible.

Daily Manna

[7] For as he thinks in his heart, so is he.

Proverbs 23:7 New Life Version (NLV)

Daily Memoir

_____
_____
_____
_____
_____
_____
_____
_____
_____
_____
_____
_____
_____
_____
_____
_____
_____
_____

DAY 99

Daily Message

Opposition gives you opportunity to WORK your faith! God's Word (that you believe in your heart and confess with your mouth) never returns void!

Daily Manna

[11] So shall My word be that goes forth out of My mouth: it shall not return to Me void [without producing any effect, useless], but it shall accomplish that which I please and purpose, and it shall prosper in the thing for which I sent it.

Isaiah 55:11 Amplified Bible (AMP)

Daily Memoir

_____
_____
_____
_____
_____
_____
_____
_____
_____
_____
_____
_____
_____
_____
_____
_____

DAY 100

Daily Message

God is faithful to make good on His Word therefore be fearless to stand on it; believing as your words align with His, you will have what you say!

Daily Manna

[11] So shall my word be that goeth forth out of my mouth: it shall not return unto me void, but it shall accomplish that which I please, and it shall prosper in the thing whereto I sent it.

Isaiah 55:11 King James Version (KJV)

Daily Memoir

_____
_____
_____
_____
_____
_____
_____
_____
_____
_____
_____
_____
_____
_____
_____
_____

DAY 101

Daily Message

God created us for greatness but we limit ourselves by speaking words contrary to what He says about us. Let His Word direct our mouths.

Daily Manna

[11] So will the words that come out of my mouth not come back empty-handed. They'll do the work I sent them to do, they'll complete the assignment I gave them.

Isaiah 55:11 The Message (MSG)

Daily Memoir

_____
_____
_____
_____
_____
_____
_____
_____
_____
_____
_____
_____
_____
_____
_____
_____
_____

DAY 102

Daily Message

Whatever you are facing is only temporary; stand firm on the Word of God, which is eternal and unfailing, and watch the situation change.

Daily Manna

[11] So will My word be which goes forth from My mouth; It will not return to Me empty, Without accomplishing what I desire, And without succeeding *in the matter* for which I sent it.

Isaiah 55:11 New American Standard Bible (NASB)

Daily Memoir

_____
_____
_____
_____
_____
_____
_____
_____
_____
_____
_____
_____
_____
_____
_____
_____

DAY 103

Daily Message

You have to get rid of the old in your closet to make room for the new. I'm talking about your thinking . . . that's the re*new*al process!

Daily Manna

[11] so is my word that goes out from my mouth: It will not return to me empty, but will accomplish what I desire and achieve the purpose for which I sent it.

Isaiah 55:11 New International Version (NIV)

Daily Memoir

_____
_____
_____
_____
_____
_____
_____
_____
_____
_____
_____
_____
_____
_____
_____
_____
_____

DAY 104

Daily Message

If God is not doing things the way you THINK He should it's time to renew your mind and get on His level! His plan is always better.

Daily Manna

[11] So shall My word be that goes forth from My mouth; It shall not return to Me void, But it shall accomplish what I please, And it shall prosper *in the thing* for which I sent it.

Isaiah 55:11 New King James Version (NKJV)

Daily Memoir

_____
_____
_____
_____
_____
_____
_____
_____
_____
_____
_____
_____
_____
_____
_____
_____

DAY 105

Daily Message

We trust God! There is no other option for the disciple but to be fully committed to standing on God's Word until we get His results.

Daily Manna

[11] It is the same with my word. I send it out, and it always produces fruit. It will accomplish all I want it to, and it will prosper everywhere I send it.

Isaiah 55:11 New Living Translation (NLT)

Daily Memoir

_____
_____
_____
_____
_____
_____
_____
_____
_____
_____
_____
_____
_____
_____
_____
_____
_____
_____

DAY 106

Daily Message

Only a fool would disregard the wisdom of God by assuming they have a better plan for their lives than the Creator does. TRUST GOD!

Daily Manna

⁵ Thus says the Lord: Cursed [with great evil] is the strong man who trusts in and relies on frail man, making weak [human] flesh his arm, and whose mind and heart turn aside from the Lord.

⁶ For he shall be like a shrub or a person naked and destitute in the desert; and he shall not see any good come, but shall dwell in the parched places in the wilderness, in an uninhabited salt land.

⁷ [Most] blessed is the man who believes in, trusts in, and relies on the Lord, and whose hope and confidence the Lord is.

⁸ For he shall be like a tree planted by the waters that spreads out its roots by the river; and it shall not see and fear when heat comes; but its leaf shall be green. It shall not be anxious and full of care in the year of drought, nor shall it cease yielding fruit.

Jeremiah 17:5-8 Amplified Bible (AMP)

Daily Memoir

_____
_____
_____
_____
_____
_____
_____

DAY 107

Daily Message

When you REALIZE God's plan is better than your own and embrace your God given purpose you will begin to walk in the blessing!

Daily Manna

⁵ Thus saith the LORD; Cursed be the man that trusteth in man, and maketh flesh his arm, and whose heart departeth from the LORD.

⁶ For he shall be like the heath in the desert, and shall not see when good cometh; but shall inhabit the parched places in the wilderness, in a salt land and not inhabited.

⁷ Blessed is the man that trusteth in the LORD, and whose hope the LORD is.

⁸ For he shall be as a tree planted by the waters, and that spreadeth out her roots by the river, and shall not see when heat cometh, but her leaf shall be green; and shall not be careful in the year of drought, neither shall cease from yielding fruit.

Jeremiah 17:5-8 King James Version (KJV)

Daily Memoir

_____

_____

_____

_____

_____

_____

_____

_____

DAY 108

Daily Message

The curse has a right to come on those who are out of the Will of God. Stay in obedience to His Will and the Blessing will protect you.

Daily Manna

[5-6] God's Message: "Cursed is the strong one who depends on mere humans, Who thinks he can make it on muscle alone and sets God aside as dead weight. He's like a tumbleweed on the prairie, out of touch with the good earth. He lives rootless and aimless in a land where nothing grows.
[7-8] "But blessed is the man who trusts me, God, the woman who sticks with God. They're like trees replanted in Eden, putting down roots near the rivers—Never a worry through the hottest of summers, never dropping a leaf, Serene and calm through droughts, bearing fresh fruit every season.

Jeremiah 17:5-8 The Message (MSG)

Daily Memoir

_____
_____
_____
_____
_____
_____
_____
_____
_____
_____
_____
_____

DAY 109

Daily Message

Telling God no is saying you trust your own wisdom and plan more than His . . . even though yours has already failed you many times in the past.

Daily Manna

⁵ Thus says the LORD, "Cursed is the man who trusts in mankind And makes flesh his strength, And whose heart turns away from the LORD.

⁶ "For he will be like a bush in the desert And will not see when prosperity comes, But will live in stony wastes in the wilderness, A land of salt without inhabitant.

⁷ "Blessed is the man who trusts in the LORD And whose trust is the LORD.

⁸ "For he will be like a tree planted by the water, That extends its roots by a stream And will not fear when the heat comes; But its leaves will be green, And it will not be anxious in a year of drought Nor cease to yield fruit.

Jeremiah 17:5-8 New American Standard Bible (NASB)

Daily Memoir

DAY 110

Daily Message

Only a FOOL embraces and boast in things that contradict the Word of God . . . sadly they foolishly walk into the path of destruction by their words.

Daily Manna

5 This is what the LORD says: "Cursed is the one who trusts in man, who draws strength from mere flesh and whose heart turns away from the LORD.

6 That person will be like a bush in the wastelands; they will not see prosperity when it comes.

They will dwell in the parched places of the desert, in a salt land where no one lives.

7 "But blessed is the one who trusts in the LORD, whose confidence is in him.

8 They will be like a tree planted by the water that sends out its roots by the stream. It does not fear when heat comes; its leaves are always green. It has no worries in a year of drought and never fails to bear fruit."

Jeremiah 17:5-8 New International Version (NIV)

Daily Memoir

_____

_____

_____

_____

_____

_____

_____

DAY 111

Daily Message

Life becomes much easier when you stop fighting with God about His plan for you. Only a fool would disagree with their Creator on why they were created.

Daily Manna

⁵ Thus says the LORD: "Cursed *is* the man who trusts in man And makes flesh his strength, Whose heart departs from the LORD.

⁶ For he shall be like a shrub in the desert, And shall not see when good comes, But shall inhabit the parched places in the wilderness, *In* a salt land *which is* not inhabited.

⁷ "Blessed *is* the man who trusts in the LORD, And whose hope is the LORD.

⁸ For he shall be like a tree planted by the waters, Which spreads out its roots by the river, And will not fear when heat comes; But its leaf will be green, And will not be anxious in the year of drought, Nor will cease from yielding fruit.

Jeremiah 17:5-8 New King James Version (NKJV)

Daily Memoir

_____
_____
_____
_____
_____
_____
_____

DAY 112

Daily Message

God is always thinking about your best interest so it would benefit you to seek His will for your life and walk in your God given purpose.

Daily Manna

⁵ This is what the LORD says: "Cursed are those who put their trust in mere humans, who rely on human strength and turn their hearts away from the LORD.
⁶ They are like stunted shrubs in the desert, with no hope for the future. They will live in the barren wilderness, in an uninhabited salty land.
⁷ "But blessed are those who trust in the LORD and have made the LORD their hope and confidence.
⁸ They are like trees planted along a riverbank, with roots that reach deep into the water. Such trees are not bothered by the heat or worried by long months of drought. Their leaves stay green, and they never stop producing fruit.

Jeremiah 17:5-8 New Living Translation (NLT)

Daily Memoir

_____
_____
_____
_____
_____
_____
_____
_____
_____

DAY 113

Daily Message

God doesn't want to be your fallback position when your plans fail. Make Him the only authority in your life because His plans always prosper.

Daily Manna

[11] For I know the thoughts and plans that I have for you, says the Lord, thoughts and plans for welfare and peace and not for evil, to give you hope in your final outcome.

Jeremiah 29:11 Amplified Bible (AMP)

Daily Memoir

_____
_____
_____
_____
_____
_____
_____
_____
_____
_____
_____
_____
_____
_____
_____
_____

DAY 114

Daily Message

God has predestined you for greatness but the choices you make will determine your destiny. Choose to walk in God's plan for your life.

Daily Manna

[11] For I know the thoughts that I think toward you, saith the LORD, thoughts of peace, and not of evil, to give you an expected end.

Jeremiah 29:11 King James Version (KJV)

Daily Memoir

_____
_____
_____
_____
_____
_____
_____
_____
_____
_____
_____
_____
_____
_____
_____
_____
_____

DAY 115

Daily Message

God's welfare plan does not include you relying on government assistance. You're too valuable to leave your care in anyone's hands but The Almighty!

Daily Manna

I know what I'm doing. I have it all planned out—plans to take care of you, not abandon you, plans to give you the future you hope for.

Jeremiah 29:11 The Message (MSG)

Daily Memoir

_____
_____
_____
_____
_____
_____
_____
_____
_____
_____
_____
_____
_____
_____
_____
_____
_____
_____

DAY 116

Daily Message

God knows why He created you and He is not second guessing His choice. You just need to trust Him with your whole heart and rely on His wisdom (direction).

Daily Manna

[11] For I know the plans that I have for you,' declares the LORD, 'plans for welfare and not for calamity to give you a future and a hope.

Jeremiah 29:11 New American Standard Bible (NASB)

Daily Memoir

_____
_____
_____
_____
_____
_____
_____
_____
_____
_____
_____
_____
_____
_____
_____
_____

DAY 117

Daily Message

This is the day the Lord has made; seek His wisdom for the plans He has for it so that you will walk in the blessing!

Daily Manna

[11] For I know the plans I have for you," declares the LORD, "plans to prosper you and not to harm you, plans to give you hope and a future.

Jeremiah 29:11 New International Version (NIV)

Daily Memoir

_____
_____
_____
_____
_____
_____
_____
_____
_____
_____
_____
_____
_____
_____
_____
_____
_____
_____

DAY 118

Daily Message

God already has a plan for you; if you put your complete trust in Him you are assured to fulfill your destiny and enjoy a good life.

Daily Manna

[11] For I know the thoughts that I think toward you, says the LORD, thoughts of peace and not of evil, to give you a future and a hope.

Jeremiah 29:11 New King James Version (NKJV)

Daily Memoir

_____
_____
_____
_____
_____
_____
_____
_____
_____
_____
_____
_____
_____
_____
_____
_____

DAY 119

Daily Message

The good life (for you) is not measuring yourself by other people's accomplishments but walking in the purpose God created specifically for you.

Daily Manna

[11] For I know the plans I have for you," says the LORD. "They are plans for good and not for disaster, to give you a future and a hope.

Jeremiah 29:11 New Living Translation (NLT)

Daily Memoir

_____
_____
_____
_____
_____
_____
_____
_____
_____
_____
_____
_____
_____
_____
_____
_____
_____
_____
_____

DAY 120

Daily Message

Let your motive be to pursue God and His Word more diligently then the things of this world and God will give you your desires and more!

Daily Manna

[33] But seek (aim at and strive after) first of all His kingdom and His righteousness (His way of doing and being right), and then all these things taken together will be given you besides.

Matthew 6:33 Amplified Bible (AMP)

Daily Memoir

_____
_____
_____
_____
_____
_____
_____
_____
_____
_____
_____
_____
_____
_____
_____
_____
_____

DAY 121

Daily Message

Only those who pursue wisdom (Christ) will have Him and all He possesses but if your primary pursuit is anything else you won't be happy.

Daily Manna

[33] But seek ye first the kingdom of God, and his righteousness; and all these things shall be added unto you.

Matthew 6:33 King James Version (KJV)

Daily Memoir

_____
_____
_____
_____
_____
_____
_____
_____
_____
_____
_____
_____
_____
_____
_____
_____
_____
_____

DAY 122

Daily Message

The Blessing is not dependent on you wanting it but your obedience to the Word. Pursue the Word and the blessings will pursue you!

Daily Manna

Steep your life in God-reality, God-initiative, God-provisions. Don't worry about missing out. You'll find all your everyday human concerns will be met.

Matthew 6:33 The Message (MSG)

Daily Memoir

_____
_____
_____
_____
_____
_____
_____
_____
_____
_____
_____
_____
_____
_____
_____

DAY 123

Daily Message

We cannot focus on the world's standard of success in God's Kingdom; seek to fulfill God's vision in the earth then success will come.

Daily Manna

[33] But seek first His kingdom and His righteousness, and all these things will be added to you.

Matthew 6:33 New American Standard Bible (NASB)

Daily Memoir

_____
_____
_____
_____
_____
_____
_____
_____
_____
_____
_____
_____
_____
_____
_____
_____
_____

DAY 124

Daily Message

You don't have to pursue God's Blessing! Simply abide in His Word, make Him the focal point of your life, and the blessings will overtake you!

Daily Manna

[33] But seek first his kingdom and his righteousness, and all these things will be given to you as well.

Matthew 6:33 New International Version (NIV)

Daily Memoir

_____

_____

_____

_____

_____

_____

_____

_____

_____

_____

_____

_____

_____

_____

_____

_____

_____

DAY 125

Daily Message

When your focus is on seeking God's Kingdom (the way God does things) and pleasing Him you don't have to look for blessings because they find you.

Daily Manna

[33] But seek first the kingdom of God and His righteousness, and all these things shall be added to you.

Matthew 6:33 New King James Version (NKJV)

Daily Memoir

_____
_____
_____
_____
_____
_____
_____
_____
_____
_____
_____
_____
_____
_____
_____
_____
_____

DAY 126

Daily Message

Whatever we value more than God will become a weight instead of a blessing. Be sure God and His Word are your #1 priority.

Daily Manna

[33] Seek the Kingdom of God above all else, and live righteously, and he will give you everything you need.

Matthew 6:33 New Living Translation (NLT)

Daily Memoir

_____

_____

_____

_____

_____

_____

_____

_____

_____

_____

_____

_____

_____

_____

_____

_____

DAY 127

Daily Message

Study the Word so that by renewing your mind in the Word (Christ) your faith will be developed to see the impossible manifested in your life.

Daily Manna

[23] And Jesus said, [You say to Me], If You can do anything? [Why,] all things can be (are possible) to him who believes!

Mark 9:23 Amplified Bible (AMP)

Daily Memoir

_____
_____
_____
_____
_____
_____
_____
_____
_____
_____
_____
_____
_____
_____
_____
_____
_____
_____

DAY 128

Daily Message

Faith in God and His Word is what cast out all fear of failure. All things are possible to those who love (obey) the Word of God.

Daily Manna

[23] Jesus said unto him, If thou canst believe, all things are possible to him that believeth.

Mark 9:23 King James Version (KJV)

Daily Memoir

_____
_____
_____
_____
_____
_____
_____
_____
_____
_____
_____
_____
_____
_____
_____
_____
_____

DAY 129

Daily Message

Without accepting what you know about God's Word and applying it to your life you are not in faith therefore will not produce the results promised.

Daily Manna

[23] Jesus said, "If? There are no 'ifs' among believers. Anything can happen."

Mark 9:23 The Message (MSG)

Daily Memoir

_____
_____
_____
_____
_____
_____
_____
_____
_____
_____
_____
_____
_____
_____
_____
_____
_____
_____

DAY 130

Daily Message

God said you are already blessed but whatever you receive is based on what you believe and confess, according to His word.

Daily Manna

²³ And Jesus said to him, "'If You can?' All things are possible to him who believes."

Mark 9:23 New American Standard Bible (NASB)

Daily Memoir

_____
_____
_____
_____
_____
_____
_____
_____
_____
_____
_____
_____
_____
_____
_____
_____
_____

DAY 131

Daily Message

The only thing impossible to God is to lie so when we take Him at His Word, believing and speaking it, all things are possible to us.

Daily Manna

²³ "'If you can'?" said Jesus. "Everything is possible for one who believes."

Mark 9:23 New International Version (NIV)

Daily Memoir

DAY 132

Daily Message

We are BLESSED (empowered to prosper) by the WORD which is IMPLANTED in us through continually HEARING it so that we INCREASE our faith to DO THE IMPOSSIBLE!

Daily Manna

[23] Jesus said to him, "If you can believe, all things *are* possible to him who believes."

Mark 9:23 New King James Version (NKJV)

Daily Memoir

_____
_____
_____
_____
_____
_____
_____
_____
_____
_____
_____
_____
_____
_____
_____
_____
_____
_____

DAY 133

Daily Message

Don't get discouraged; seek God's wisdom on the situation and know that abiding in God's wisdom makes all things possible to you!

Daily Manna

[23] "What do you mean, 'If I can'?" Jesus asked. "Anything is possible if a person believes."

Mark 9:23 New Living Translation (NLT)

Daily Memoir

_____
_____
_____
_____
_____
_____
_____
_____
_____
_____
_____
_____
_____
_____
_____
_____
_____

DAY 134

Daily Message

The vision God has for you cannot fit in a box so you must take the limits off your mind to believe God for those things that seem impossible.

Daily Manna

[27] Jesus glanced around at them and said, With men [it is] impossible, but not with God; for all things are possible with God.

Mark 10:27 Amplified Bible (AMP)

Daily Memoir

_____
_____
_____
_____
_____
_____
_____
_____
_____
_____
_____
_____
_____
_____
_____
_____
_____
_____

DAY 135

Daily Message

God is able to do the impossible and as long as you abide (continue, dwell, remain, stay) in Him (the Word) so can you! Believe the Word!

Daily Manna

[27] And Jesus looking upon them saith, With men it is impossible, but not with God: for with God all things are possible.

Mark 10:27 King James Version (KJV)

Daily Memoir

_____
_____
_____
_____
_____
_____
_____
_____
_____
_____
_____
_____
_____
_____
_____
_____

DAY 136

Daily Message

Do not forfeit the Power God has put in you! Abide in the Word of God; keep speaking it and believe ALL THINGS ARE POSSIBLE WITH CHRIST (YOUR POWER SOURCE) IN YOU!

Daily Manna

[27] Jesus was blunt: "No chance at all if you think you can pull it off by yourself. Every chance in the world if you let God do it."

Mark 10:27 The Message (MSG)

Daily Memoir

_____
_____
_____
_____
_____
_____
_____
_____
_____
_____
_____
_____
_____
_____
_____
_____

DAY 137

Daily Message

Christ has set you free from ALL things; the only limitations you face are those you have put on yourself. Renew your mind in the Word to accomplish the impossible!

Daily Manna

[27] Looking at them, Jesus said, "With people it is impossible, but not with God; for all things are possible with God."

Mark 10:27 New American Standard Bible (NASB)

Daily Memoir

_____

_____

_____

_____

_____

_____

_____

_____

_____

_____

_____

_____

_____

_____

_____

_____

_____

DAY 138

Daily Message

Unless you're consistently hearing the Word you won't know it but it takes more than just knowing . . . if you don't believe the Word, you say you know, you won't accomplish the impossible!

Daily Manna

[27] Jesus looked at them and said, "With man this is impossible, but not with God; all things are possible with God."

Mark 10:27 New International Version (NIV)

Daily Memoir

_____
_____
_____
_____
_____
_____
_____
_____
_____
_____
_____
_____
_____
_____
_____
_____
_____

DAY 139

Daily Message

We can't accomplish the great works God has called us to without first acknowledging Him as our Great God, in Who all things are possible.

Daily Manna

[27] But Jesus looked at them and said, "With men *it is* impossible, but not with God; for with God all things are possible."

Mark 10:27 New King James Version (NKJV)

Daily Memoir

_____

_____

_____

_____

_____

_____

_____

_____

_____

_____

_____

_____

_____

_____

_____

_____

_____

DAY 140

Daily Message

We have been created in the image of Christ to do the impossible but unless we abide in His wisdom we will never accomplish that dream we see as bigger than our own capabilities.

Daily Manna

[27] Jesus looked at them intently and said, "Humanly speaking, it is impossible. But not with God. Everything is possible with God."

Mark 10:27 New Living Translation (NLT)

Daily Memoir

_____

_____

_____

_____

_____

_____

_____

_____

_____

_____

_____

_____

_____

_____

_____

_____

DAY 141

Daily Message

What are you expecting God to do today? Anticipation and Expectation will cause you to rejoice NOW before you see your Manifestation!

Daily Manna

[24] For this reason I am telling you, whatever you ask for in prayer, believe (trust and be confident) that it is granted to you, and you will [get it].

Mark 11:24 Amplified Bible (AMP)

Daily Memoir

_____
_____
_____
_____
_____
_____
_____
_____
_____
_____
_____
_____
_____
_____
_____
_____
_____
_____

DAY 142

Daily Message

God has already said what the end shall be now we just have to mimic His Words and give Him continual thanks that it is done!

Daily Manna

[24] Therefore I say unto you, What things soever ye desire, when ye pray, believe that ye receive them, and ye shall have them.

Mark 11:24 King James Version (KJV)

Daily Memoir

_____
_____
_____
_____
_____
_____
_____
_____
_____
_____
_____
_____
_____
_____
_____
_____
_____
_____

DAY 143

Daily Message

Knowing is only important in the context that we believe what we know; it is our continual belief of God's Word and speaking it that get results!

Daily Manna

That's why I urge you to pray for absolutely everything, ranging from small to large. Include everything as you embrace this God-life, and you'll get God's everything.

Mark 11:24 The Message (MSG)

Daily Memoir

_____
_____
_____
_____
_____
_____
_____
_____
_____
_____
_____
_____
_____
_____
_____
_____

DAY 144

Daily Message

Faith is the exchange for those things you desire from God. The Word gives hope and by ABIDING in the Word you produce faith to receive what you are asking for!

Daily Manna

[24] Therefore I say to you, all things for which you pray and ask, believe that you have received them, and they will be *granted* you.

Mark 11:24 New American Standard Bible (NASB)

Daily Memoir

_____
_____
_____
_____
_____
_____
_____
_____
_____
_____
_____
_____
_____
_____
_____
_____
_____

DAY 145

Daily Message

All things are possible with God (the Word). Remove the boundaries of limited thinking through meditating on the Word of God and allowing Him to take root in you and uproot the unbelief.

Daily Manna

[24] Therefore I tell you, whatever you ask for in prayer, believe that you have received it, and it will be yours.

Mark 11:24 New International Version (NIV)

Daily Memoir

_____
_____
_____
_____
_____
_____
_____
_____
_____
_____
_____
_____
_____
_____
_____
_____

DAY 146

Daily Message

The only limits that can stop you are in the boundaries of your mind. Therefore renew your mind through God's Word to enlarge your territory. NO LIMITS!

Daily Manna

[24] Therefore I say to you, whatever things you ask when you pray, believe that you receive *them,* and you will have *them.*

Mark 11:24 New King James Version (NKJV)

Daily Memoir

_____
_____
_____
_____
_____
_____
_____
_____
_____
_____
_____
_____
_____
_____
_____
_____

DAY 147

Daily Message

We are only limited by what we don't know or believe in the Word. Make a decision to know and believe the Word and take the limits off!

Daily Manna

[24] I tell you, you can pray for anything, and if you believe that you've received it, it will be yours.

Mark 11:24 New Living Translation (NLT)

Daily Memoir

_____
_____
_____
_____
_____
_____
_____
_____
_____
_____
_____
_____
_____
_____
_____
_____
_____
_____

DAY 148

Daily Message

Since we were made to be like God we should be seeking His will and purpose for us instead of seeking to fulfill our personal goals.

Daily Manna

[30] I am able to do nothing from Myself [independently, of My own accord—but only as I am taught by God and as I get His orders]. Even as I hear, I judge [I decide as I am bidden to decide. As the voice comes to Me, so I give a decision], and My judgment is right (just, righteous), because I do not seek or consult My own will [I have no desire to do what is pleasing to Myself, My own aim, My own purpose] but only the will and pleasure of the Father Who sent Me.

John 5:30 Amplified Bible (AMP)

Daily Memoir

_____

_____

_____

_____

_____

_____

_____

_____

_____

_____

_____

_____

DAY 149

Daily Message

As believers we don't seek the blessing; we seek to please God by making sure our lives are aligned with the Word, and then the blessing will seek us.

Daily Manna

[30] I can of mine own self do nothing: as I hear, I judge: and my judgment is just; because I seek not mine own will, but the will of the Father which hath sent me.

John 5:30 King James Version (KJV)

Daily Memoir

_____
_____
_____
_____
_____
_____
_____
_____
_____
_____
_____
_____
_____
_____
_____
_____

DAY 150

Daily Message

Getting outside the will of God only causes stress and frustration. God promises you the desires of your heart as you seek Him and abide in His will for you.

Daily Manna

I can't do a solitary thing on my own: I listen, then I decide. You can trust my decision because I'm not out to get my own way but only to carry out orders.

John 5:30 The Message (MSG)

Daily Memoir

_____
_____
_____
_____
_____
_____
_____
_____
_____
_____
_____
_____
_____
_____
_____

DAY 151

Daily Message

You are more blessed than you know so aspire to have more than material things, cars, houses, and money. God wants to use to bless nations!

Daily Manna

[30] "I can do nothing on My own initiative. As I hear, I judge; and My judgment is just, because I do not seek My own will, but the will of Him who sent Me.

John 5:30 New American Standard Bible (NASB)

Daily Memoir

DAY 152

Daily Message

You have to be rich! Not so you can buy more things, but other people's lives depend on you to be an asset to the Kingdom not just collect assets for yourself.

Daily Manna

[30] By myself I can do nothing; I judge only as I hear, and my judgment is just, for I seek not to please myself but him who sent me.

John 5:30 New International Version (NIV)

Daily Memoir

DAY 153

Daily Message

Confess: I am blessed (fruitful and multiplying and replenishing and subduing the earth and exercising dominion) and in ME all the families of the earth will be blessed!

Daily Manna

[30] I can of Myself do nothing. As I hear, I judge; and My judgment is righteous, because I do not seek My own will but the will of the Father who sent Me.

John 5:30 New King James Version (NKJV)

Daily Memoir

_____

_____

_____

_____

_____

_____

_____

_____

_____

_____

_____

_____

_____

_____

_____

DAY 154

Daily Message

God didn't say you should not want things; He said do not make things your focus. Set your heart on doing the Word of God and He will bring those things to you.

Daily Manna

[30] I can do nothing on my own. I judge as God tells me. Therefore, my judgment is just, because I carry out the will of the one who sent me, not my own will.

John 5:30 New Living Translation (NLT)

Daily Memoir

_____
_____
_____
_____
_____
_____
_____
_____
_____
_____
_____
_____
_____
_____
_____
_____

DAY 155

Daily Message

The struggle is over! Jesus did all the hard work to make us free from the curse we just have to believe His Word and praise Him!

Daily Manna

³¹ So Jesus said to those Jews who had believed in Him, If you abide in My word [hold fast to My teachings and live in accordance with them], you are truly My disciples.

³² And you will know the Truth, and the Truth will set you free.

John 8:31-32 Amplified Bible (AMP)

Daily Memoir

_____
_____
_____
_____
_____
_____
_____
_____
_____
_____
_____
_____
_____
_____
_____

DAY 156

Daily Message

The key to being a disciple is saying Yes to God's will; freedom is found in your YES!

Daily Manna

[31] Then said Jesus to those Jews which believed on him, If ye continue in my word, then are ye my disciples indeed;
[32] And ye shall know the truth, and the truth shall make you free.

John 8:31-32 King James Version (KJV)

Daily Memoir

_____
_____
_____
_____
_____
_____
_____
_____
_____
_____
_____
_____
_____
_____
_____
_____
_____

DAY 157

Daily Message

If we have God's Word implanted in our hearts nothing is impossible! It's His Word that we believe (act on) that brings freedom!

Daily Manna

31-32 Then Jesus turned to the Jews who had claimed to believe in him. "If you stick with this, living out what I tell you, you are my disciples for sure. Then you will experience for yourselves the truth, and the truth will free you."

John 8:31-32 The Message (MSG)

Daily Memoir

_____
_____
_____
_____
_____
_____
_____
_____
_____
_____
_____
_____
_____
_____
_____
_____
_____

DAY 158

Daily Message

Either you believe the Word of God or you don't. Either way it doesn't change the fact that it's TRUE and it's the truth you know and believe that makes you free.

Daily Manna

[31] So Jesus was saying to those Jews who had believed Him, "If you continue in My word, *then* you are truly disciples of Mine; [32] and you will know the truth, and the truth will make you free."

John 8:31-32 New American Standard Bible (NASB)

Daily Memoir

_____
_____
_____
_____
_____
_____
_____
_____
_____
_____
_____
_____
_____
_____
_____
_____
_____

DAY 159

Daily Message

Society says be open-minded to others beliefs. BUT any belief not based on God's Word brings bondage; the Word brings FREEDOM!

Daily Manna

[31] To the Jews who had believed him, Jesus said, "If you hold to my teaching, you are really my disciples. [32] Then you will know the truth, and the truth will set you free."

John 8:31-32 New International Version (NIV)

Daily Memoir

_____
_____
_____
_____
_____
_____
_____
_____
_____
_____
_____
_____
_____
_____
_____
_____
_____

DAY 160

Daily Message

As Christ's disciples we must get out of our own way to be stretched beyond our comfort zone so we may lay down our lives for the Kingdom!

Daily Manna

[31] Then Jesus said to those Jews who believed Him, "If you abide in My word, you are My disciples indeed. [32] And you shall know the truth, and the truth shall make you free."

John 8:31-32 New King James Version (NKJV)

Daily Memoir

_____
_____
_____
_____
_____
_____
_____
_____
_____
_____
_____
_____
_____
_____
_____
_____
_____

DAY 161

Daily Message

We have been freed from everything that comes with the curse but unless we embrace what Christ did we will expect and accept defeat.

Daily Manna

³¹ Jesus said to the people who believed in him, "You are truly my disciples if you remain faithful to my teachings. ³² And you will know the truth, and the truth will set you free."

John 8:31-32 New Living Translation (NLT)

Daily Memoir

_____
_____
_____
_____
_____
_____
_____
_____
_____
_____
_____
_____
_____
_____
_____
_____

DAY 162

Daily Message

When we abide in God's wisdom our paths become sweat less! His plan is not that life would be hard but that we would enjoy life in Him!

Daily Manna

The thief comes only in order to steal and kill and destroy. I came that they may have and enjoy life, and have it in abundance (to the full, till it overflows).

John 10:10 Amplified Bible (AMP)

Daily Memoir

_____

_____

_____

_____

_____

_____

_____

_____

_____

_____

_____

_____

_____

_____

DAY 163

Daily Message

When God is the Owner and Master of our lives He establishes His plan and purpose so that we may obtain and maintain the good life!

Daily Manna

[10] The thief cometh not, but for to steal, and to kill, and to destroy: I am come that they might have life, and that they might have it more abundantly.

John 10:10 King James Version (KJV)

Daily Memoir

_____
_____
_____
_____
_____
_____
_____
_____
_____
_____
_____
_____
_____
_____
_____
_____
_____
_____

DAY 164

Daily Message

Without Christ we cannot live; we can only exist in death. It is through abiding in the Word of God that we obtain life . . . in abundance!

Daily Manna

A thief is only there to steal and kill and destroy. I came so they can have real and eternal life, more and better life than they ever dreamed of.

John 10:10 The Message (MSG)

Daily Memoir

_____
_____
_____
_____
_____
_____
_____
_____
_____
_____
_____
_____
_____
_____
_____
_____
_____
_____

DAY 165

Daily Message

Life is not hard when you choose the life that Christ has for you! Make the decision to submit to His Word so you can walk in the Blessing!

Daily Manna

[10] The thief comes only to steal and kill and destroy; I came that they may have life, and have *it* abundantly.

John 10:10 New American Standard Bible (NASB)

Daily Memoir

_____
_____
_____
_____
_____
_____
_____
_____
_____
_____
_____
_____
_____
_____
_____
_____
_____
_____

DAY 166

Daily Message

We are set apart from the world by renewing our mind through the Word of Christ and abiding in His Word so that we live the abundant life.

Daily Manna

[10] The thief comes only to steal and kill and destroy; I have come that they may have life, and have it to the full.

John 10:10 New International Version (NIV)

Daily Memoir

_____

_____

_____

_____

_____

_____

_____

_____

_____

_____

_____

_____

_____

_____

_____

_____

DAY 167

Daily Message

You are still alive so Satan's plan to destroy you didn't work! Get up, shake yourself and take hold of the abundant life and purpose God has for you!

Daily Manna

[10] The thief does not come except to steal, and to kill, and to destroy. I have come that they may have life, and that they may have *it* more abundantly.

John 10:10 New King James Version (NKJV)

Daily Memoir

_____
_____
_____
_____
_____
_____
_____
_____
_____
_____
_____
_____
_____
_____
_____
_____
_____
_____

DAY 168

Daily Message

Discipleship will cost you your life but life in Christ produces the good life! Commit to not only making Him your Savior but your Lord (Master and Owner) also.

Daily Manna

[10] The thief's purpose is to steal and kill and destroy. My purpose is to give them a rich and satisfying life.

John 10:10 New Living Translation (NLT)

Daily Memoir

_____
_____
_____
_____
_____
_____
_____
_____
_____
_____
_____
_____
_____
_____
_____
_____

DAY 169

Daily Message

Jesus came so we can fellowship with the Father. Our pastors teach us 'how to' fellowship but it's still our responsibility to do it.

Daily Manna

[17] If you know these things, blessed and happy and to be envied are you if you practice them [if you act accordingly and really do them].

John 13:17 Amplified Bible (AMP)

Daily Memoir

_____
_____
_____
_____
_____
_____
_____
_____
_____
_____
_____
_____
_____
_____
_____
_____

DAY 170

Daily Message

Stay focused on the most recent instruction God has given you; succeed in accomplishing that and God will trust you with more.

Daily Manna

[17] If ye know these things, happy are ye if ye do them.

John 13:17 King James Version (KJV)

Daily Memoir

_____

_____

_____

_____

_____

_____

_____

_____

_____

_____

_____

_____

_____

_____

_____

_____

_____

DAY 171

Daily Message

You can trust that God will entrust you with more when He can trust you to be obedient with what He has already given you.

Daily Manna

If you understand what I'm telling you, act like it—and live a blessed life.

John 13:17 The Message (MSG)

Daily Memoir

_____
_____
_____
_____
_____
_____
_____
_____
_____
_____
_____
_____
_____
_____
_____
_____
_____
_____

DAY 172

Daily Message

A Disciple willingly submits to and obeys God's word at all times. We are not disciples because we say so but because we live as such.

Daily Manna

[17] If you know these things, you are blessed if you do them.

John 13:17 New American Standard Bible (NASB)

Daily Memoir

_____

_____

_____

_____

_____

_____

_____

_____

_____

_____

_____

_____

_____

_____

_____

_____

_____

_____

DAY 173

Daily Message

God requires accountability; if you won't obey the last simple instruction He gave you He will never be able to use you for anything else.

Daily Manna

[17] Now that you know these things, you will be blessed if you do them.

John 13:17 New International Version (NIV)

Daily Memoir

_____

_____

_____

_____

_____

_____

_____

_____

_____

_____

_____

_____

_____

_____

_____

_____

_____

_____

DAY 174

Daily Message

The level of honor (respect/esteem) you give to God and His Word (His Wisdom) will produce the amount of honor He will give to you.

Daily Manna

[17] If you know these things, blessed are you if you do them.

John 13:17 New King James Version (NKJV)

Daily Memoir

_____
_____
_____
_____
_____
_____
_____
_____
_____
_____
_____
_____
_____
_____
_____
_____
_____
_____

DAY 175

Daily Message

You don't just fall in to the blessing you have to walk in it on purpose by abiding (continuing, dwelling, remaining and staying) in the Word.

Daily Manna

[17] Now that you know these things, God will bless you for doing them.

John 13:17 New Living Translation (NLT)

Daily Memoir

_____

_____

_____

_____

_____

_____

_____

_____

_____

_____

_____

_____

_____

_____

_____

_____

_____

_____

DAY 176

Daily Message

God's Word sets the standard of integrity. As disciples' of Christ we are mandated, by Love Himself, to rise to the standard without excuses.

Daily Manna

[15] If you [really] love Me, you will keep (obey) My commands.

John 14:15 Amplified Bible (AMP)

Daily Memoir

_____
_____
_____
_____
_____
_____
_____
_____
_____
_____
_____
_____
_____
_____
_____
_____
_____
_____

DAY 177

Daily Message

Walking in your destiny is not merely based on God's love for you but your love (obedience) of His Word and submitting your will to His purpose!

Daily Manna

[15] If ye love me, keep my commandments.

John 14:15 King James Version (KJV)

Daily Memoir

_____
_____
_____
_____
_____
_____
_____
_____
_____
_____
_____
_____
_____
_____
_____
_____
_____
_____

DAY 178

Daily Message

Love is obeying all of God's instructions no matter how you feel about it. It is this act of love that proves we are His disciples.

Daily Manna

[15] If you love me, show it by doing what I've told you.

John 14:15 The Message (MSG)

Daily Memoir

_____
_____
_____
_____
_____
_____
_____
_____
_____
_____
_____
_____
_____
_____
_____
_____
_____
_____

DAY 179

Daily Message

When you love God you will not compromise His word to fulfill your desires. Loving God is not in what you say but what you do . . . DO the Word!

Daily Manna

[15] "If you love Me, you will keep My commandments.

John 14:15 New American Standard Bible (NASB)

Daily Memoir

_____

_____

_____

_____

_____

_____

_____

_____

_____

_____

_____

_____

_____

_____

_____

_____

_____

DAY 180

Daily Message

We don't obey God to make Him love us; He already loves us more than we can comprehend. We obey God because we love Him point blank.

Daily Manna

[15] "If you love me, keep my commands.

John 14:15 New International Version (NIV)

Daily Memoir

_____
_____
_____
_____
_____
_____
_____
_____
_____
_____
_____
_____
_____
_____
_____
_____
_____
_____

DAY 181

Daily Message

Confess: I love (obey) the Lord therefore things always work together for MY GOOD! PROMOTION/INCREASE IS ON ME! GLORY TO GOD!

Daily Manna

[15] "If you love Me, keep My commandments.

John 14:15 New King James Version (NKJV)

Daily Memoir

DAY 182

Daily Message

Don't be the one who says 'I love YOU Lord' with your mouth while your heart is far from Him. LOVE=OBEDIENCE

Daily Manna

[15] "If you love me, obey my commandments.

John 14:15 New Living Translation (NLT)

Daily Memoir

_____
_____
_____
_____
_____
_____
_____
_____
_____
_____
_____
_____
_____
_____
_____
_____
_____
_____

DAY 183

Daily Message

You cannot walk in the blessing without walking in obedience to God's Word; it is only through abiding in the Word that you can ask whatever you want.

Daily Manna

[5] I am the Vine; you are the branches. Whoever lives in Me and I in him bears much (abundant) fruit. However, apart from Me [cut off from vital union with Me] you can do nothing.

[6] If a person does not dwell in Me, he is thrown out like a [broken-off] branch, and withers; such branches are gathered up and thrown into the fire, and they are burned.

[7] If you live in Me [abide vitally united to Me] and My words remain in you and continue to live in your hearts, ask whatever you will, and it shall be done for you.

[8] When you bear (produce) much fruit, My Father is honored and glorified, and you show and prove yourselves to be true followers of Mine.

John 15:5-8 Amplified Bible (AMP)

Daily Memoir

_____

_____

_____

_____

_____

_____

DAY 184

Daily Message

God doesn't want you to lack any good thing but to receive that Promise you have to make Him the Lord of your life by submitting to His Word.

Daily Manna

⁵ I am the vine, ye are the branches: He that abideth in me, and I in him, the same bringeth forth much fruit: for without me ye can do nothing.

⁶ If a man abide not in me, he is cast forth as a branch, and is withered; and men gather them, and cast them into the fire, and they are burned.

⁷ If ye abide in me, and my words abide in you, ye shall ask what ye will, and it shall be done unto you.

⁸ Herein is my Father glorified, that ye bear much fruit; so shall ye be my disciples.

John 15:5-8 King James Version (KJV)

Daily Memoir

_____
_____
_____
_____
_____
_____
_____
_____
_____
_____
_____
_____

DAY 185

Daily Message

We are promised sweat less victory in Christ but we still must put forth effort to obtain the Promise by abiding in His Word.

Daily Manna

5-8 "I am the Vine, you are the branches. When you're joined with me and I with you, the relation intimate and organic, the harvest is sure to be abundant. Separated, you can't produce a thing. Anyone who separates from me is deadwood, gathered up and thrown on the bonfire. But if you make yourselves at home with me and my words are at home in you, you can be sure that whatever you ask will be listened to and acted upon. This is how my Father shows who he is—when you produce grapes, when you mature as my disciples.

John 15:5-8 The Message (MSG)

Daily Memoir

_____
_____
_____
_____
_____
_____
_____
_____
_____
_____

DAY 186

Daily Message

In order to walk in faith we must first abide and obey the Word of God. Faith is dependent on our trust of His Word.

Daily Manna

[5] I am the vine, you are the branches; he who abides in Me and I in him, he bears much fruit, for apart from Me you can do nothing. [6] If anyone does not abide in Me, he is thrown away as a branch and dries up; and they gather them, and cast them into the fire and they are burned. [7] If you abide in Me, and My words abide in you, ask whatever you wish, and it will be done for you. [8] My Father is glorified by this, that you bear much fruit, and *so* prove to be My disciples.

John 15:5-8 New American Standard Bible (NASB)

Daily Memoir

_____
_____
_____
_____
_____
_____
_____
_____
_____
_____
_____
_____

DAY 187

Daily Message

God's glory is manifested in us as we continue to let His Word abide and grow in us! You can never have too much of God's Word!

Daily Manna

[5] "I am the vine; you are the branches. If you remain in me and I in you, you will bear much fruit; apart from me you can do nothing. [6] If you do not remain in me, you are like a branch that is thrown away and withers; such branches are picked up, thrown into the fire and burned. [7] If you remain in me and my words remain in you, ask whatever you wish, and it will be done for you. [8] This is to my Father's glory, that you bear much fruit, showing yourselves to be my disciples.

John 15:5-8 New International Version (NIV)

Daily Memoir

_____
_____
_____
_____
_____
_____
_____
_____
_____
_____
_____
_____

DAY 188

Daily Message

God does not take back any promise He has made therefore it must come to pass for those who remain unmovable in His Word!

Daily Manna

[5] "I am the vine, you *are* the branches. He who abides in Me, and I in him, bears much fruit; for without Me you can do nothing. [6] If anyone does not abide in Me, he is cast out as a branch and is withered; and they gather them and throw *them* into the fire, and they are burned. [7] If you abide in Me, and My words abide in you, you will ask what you desire, and it shall be done for you. [8] By this My Father is glorified, that you bear much fruit; so you will be My disciples.

John 15:5-8 New King James Version (NKJV)

Daily Memoir

DAY 189

Daily Message

God never changes. He is faithful to fulfill His Word. Therefore if we abide in His Word and allow it to abide in us the promise can't be stopped from being fulfilled!

Daily Manna

⁵ "Yes, I am the vine; you are the branches. Those who remain in me, and I in them, will produce much fruit. For apart from me you can do nothing. ⁶ Anyone who does not remain in me is thrown away like a useless branch and withers. Such branches are gathered into a pile to be burned. ⁷ But if you remain in me and my words remain in you, you may ask for anything you want, and it will be granted! ⁸ When you produce much fruit, you are my true disciples. This brings great glory to my Father.

John 15:5-8 New Living Translation (NLT)

Daily Memoir

_____

_____

_____

_____

_____

_____

_____

_____

_____

_____

DAY 190

Daily Message

Don't allow circumstances to define you, you are more than a conqueror so open your mouth and say what the Word says about you.

Daily Manna

[17] As it is written, I have made you the father of many nations. [He was appointed our father] in the sight of God in Whom he believed, Who gives life to the dead and speaks of the nonexistent things that [He has foretold and promised] as if they [already] existed.

[18] [For Abraham, human reason for] hope being gone, hoped in faith that he should become the father of many nations, as he had been promised, So [numberless] shall your descendants be.

[19] He did not weaken in faith when he considered the [utter] impotence of his own body, which was as good as dead because he was about a hundred years old, or [when he considered] the barrenness of Sarah's [deadened] womb.

[20] No unbelief or distrust made him waver (doubtingly question) concerning the promise of God, but he grew strong and was empowered by faith as he gave praise and glory to God,

[21] Fully satisfied and assured that God was able and mighty to keep His word and to do what He had promised.

Romans 4:17-21 Amplified Bible (AMP)

Daily Memoir

_____

_____

_____

DAY 191

Daily Message

We are not limited to circumstances; if we change the way we speak we will change what we see to the thing which we believe.

Daily Manna

[17] (As it is written, I have made thee a father of many nations,) before him whom he believed, even God, who quickeneth the dead, and calleth those things which be not as though they were.

[18] Who against hope believed in hope, that he might become the father of many nations, according to that which was spoken, So shall thy seed be.

[19] And being not weak in faith, he considered not his own body now dead, when he was about an hundred years old, neither yet the deadness of Sarah's womb:

[20] He staggered not at the promise of God through unbelief; but was strong in faith, giving glory to God;

[21] And being fully persuaded that, what he had promised, he was able also to perform.

Romans 4:17-21 King James Version (KJV)

Daily Memoir

_____

_____

_____

_____

_____

_____

_____

DAY 192

Daily Message

Don't let the situation speak the outcome! The words you speak create your outcome so open your mouth and say what God has said about it.

Daily Manna

[17-18] We call Abraham "father" not because he got God's attention by living like a saint, but because God made something out of Abraham when he was a nobody. Isn't that what we've always read in Scripture, God saying to Abraham, "I set you up as father of many peoples"? Abraham was first named "father" and then became a father because he dared to trust God to do what only God could do: raise the dead to life, with a word make something out of nothing. When everything was hopeless, Abraham believed anyway, deciding to live not on the basis of what he saw he couldn't do but on what God said he would do. And so he was made father of a multitude of peoples. God himself said to him, "You're going to have a big family, Abraham!"

[19-21] Abraham didn't focus on his own impotence and say, "It's hopeless. This hundred-year-old body could never father a child." Nor did he survey Sarah's decades of infertility and give up. He didn't tiptoe around God's promise asking cautiously skeptical questions. He plunged into the promise and came up strong, ready for God, sure that God would make good on what he had said.

Romans 4:17-21 The Message (MSG)

Daily Memoir

_____

_____

_____

_____

DAY 193

Daily Message

We don't wait for the situation to change before we praise God; we do it RIGHT NOW because we are fully persuaded it must line up with His Word!

Daily Manna

[17] (as it is written, "A FATHER OF MANY NATIONS HAVE I MADE YOU") in the presence of Him whom he believed, *even* God, who gives life to the dead and calls into being that which does not exist. [18] In hope against hope he believed, so that he might become a father of many nations according to that which had been spoken, "SO SHALL YOUR DESCENDANTS BE." [19] Without becoming weak in faith he contemplated his own body, now as good as dead since he was about a hundred years old, and the deadness of Sarah's womb; [20] yet, with respect to the promise of God, he did not waver in unbelief but grew strong in faith, giving glory to God, [21] and being fully assured that what God had promised, He was able also to perform.

Romans 4:17-21 New American Standard Bible (NASB)

Daily Memoir

_____
_____
_____
_____
_____
_____
_____
_____

DAY 194

Daily Message

God is faithful to do what He promised for those who are faithful to abide, continue, dwell, remain, and stay fully persuaded in His Word. Is that you?

Daily Manna

[17] As it is written: "I have made you a father of many nations." He is our father in the sight of God, in whom he believed—the God who gives life to the dead and calls into being things that were not.
[18] Against all hope, Abraham in hope believed and so became the father of many nations, just as it had been said to him, "So shall your offspring be."
[19] Without weakening in his faith, he faced the fact that his body was as good as dead—since he was about a hundred years old—and that Sarah's womb was also dead. [20] Yet he did not waver through unbelief regarding the promise of God, but was strengthened in his faith and gave glory to God, [21] being fully persuaded that God had power to do what he had promised.

Romans 4:17-21 New International Version (NIV)

Daily Memoir

_____
_____
_____
_____
_____
_____
_____
_____
_____

DAY 195

Daily Message

You're only limited by what you choose to believe; choose to believe what God's word says about you and walk in the blessing!

Daily Manna

[17] (as it is written, *"I have made you a father of many nations"*) in the presence of Him whom he believed—God, who gives life to the dead and calls those things which do not exist as though they did; [18] who, contrary to hope, in hope believed, so that he became the father of many nations, according to what was spoken, *"So shall your descendants be."* [19] And not being weak in faith, he did not consider his own body, already dead (since he was about a hundred years old), and the deadness of Sarah's womb. [20] He did not waver at the promise of God through unbelief, but was strengthened in faith, giving glory to God, [21] and being fully convinced that what He had promised He was also able to perform.

Romans 4:17-21 New King James Version (NKJV)

Daily Memoir

DAY 196

Daily Message

ALL THINGS are possible (can be) to those who constantly remain fully persuaded and convinced in the power of God's Word that works in us.

Daily Manna

[17] That is what the Scriptures mean when God told him, "I have made you the father of many nations." This happened because Abraham believed in the God who brings the dead back to life and who creates new things out of nothing.

[18] Even when there was no reason for hope, Abraham kept hoping—believing that he would become the father of many nations. For God had said to him, "That's how many descendants you will have!"

[19] And Abraham's faith did not weaken, even though, at about 100 years of age, he figured his body was as good as dead—and so was Sarah's womb.

[20] Abraham never wavered in believing God's promise. In fact, his faith grew stronger, and in this he brought glory to God. [21] He was fully convinced that God is able to do whatever he promises.

Romans 4:17-21 New Living Translation (NLT)

Daily Memoir

_____

_____

_____

_____

_____

_____

_____

DAY 197

Daily Message

God loves us; we know it but once we really believe it nothing will be impossible for us. We are Victorious!

Daily Manna

[37] Yet amid all these things we are more than conquerors and gain a surpassing victory through Him Who loved us. [38] For I am persuaded beyond doubt (am sure) that neither death nor life, nor angels nor principalities, nor things impending and threatening nor things to come, nor powers, [39] Nor height nor depth, nor anything else in all creation will be able to separate us from the love of God which is in Christ Jesus our Lord.

Romans 8:37-39 Amplified Bible (AMP)

Daily Memoir

_____

_____

_____

_____

_____

_____

_____

_____

_____

_____

_____

_____

_____

DAY 198

Daily Message

Don't be a victim of circumstance. Believe you are more than a conquer so you will be empowered to walk in victory through Christ! Whatever you speak forth shall come to pass!

Daily Manna

[37] Nay, in all these things we are more than conquerors through him that loved us. [38] For I am persuaded, that neither death, nor life, nor angels, nor principalities, nor powers, nor things present, nor things to come, [39] Nor height, nor depth, nor any other creature, shall be able to separate us from the love of God, which is in Christ Jesus our Lord.

Romans 8:37-39 King James Version (KJV)

Daily Memoir

_____

_____

_____

_____

_____

_____

_____

_____

_____

_____

_____

_____

_____

DAY 199

Daily Message

Anyone born of God CANNOT FAIL! You have been endowed with supernatural power to be great! Don't be afraid. YOU ALWAYS WIN!!!

Daily Manna

[37-39] None of this fazes us because Jesus loves us. I'm absolutely convinced that nothing—nothing living or dead, angelic or demonic, today or tomorrow, high or low, thinkable or unthinkable—absolutely nothing can get between us and God's love because of the way that Jesus our Master has embraced us.

Romans 8:37-39 The Message (MSG)

Daily Memoir

_____
_____
_____
_____
_____
_____
_____
_____
_____
_____
_____
_____
_____
_____
_____

DAY 200

Daily Message

The key to receiving all things is to believe God loves you and because of that love Christ gave His life to make all things available to you!

Daily Manna

[37] But in all these things we overwhelmingly conquer through Him who loved us. [38] For I am convinced that neither death, nor life, nor angels, nor principalities, nor things present, nor things to come, nor powers, [39] nor height, nor depth, nor any other created thing, will be able to separate us from the love of God, which is in Christ Jesus our Lord.

Romans 8:37-39 New American Standard Bible (NASB)

Daily Memoir

_____
_____
_____
_____
_____
_____
_____
_____
_____
_____
_____
_____
_____
_____

DAY 201

Daily Message

The only thing impossible for God to do is fail therefore when we put our complete trust in Him we always triumph as more than conquerors!

Daily Manna

[37] No, in all these things we are more than conquerors through him who loved us. [38] For I am convinced that neither death nor life, neither angels nor demons, neither the present nor the future, nor any powers, [39] neither height nor depth, nor anything else in all creation, will be able to separate us from the love of God that is in Christ Jesus our Lord.

Romans 8:37-39 New International Version (NIV)

Daily Memoir

_____

_____

_____

_____

_____

_____

_____

_____

_____

_____

_____

_____

DAY 202

Daily Message

God created you to win THEN placed you in the Earth! You are more than capable (through the Blood) to conquer any challenge that comes your way!

Daily Manna

[37] Yet in all these things we are more than conquerors through Him who loved us. [38] For I am persuaded that neither death nor life, nor angels nor principalities nor powers, nor things present nor things to come, [39] nor height nor depth, nor any other created thing, shall be able to separate us from the love of God which is in Christ Jesus our Lord.

Romans 8:37-39 New King James Version (NKJV)

Daily Memoir

_____

_____

_____

_____

_____

_____

_____

_____

_____

_____

_____

_____

DAY 203

Daily Message

The enemy brings attacks to break your praise. You have to make the decision to praise God in spite of what you see. Victory is a mindset! Have a PRAISE BREAK! Glory to God!

Daily Manna

[37] No, despite all these things, overwhelming victory is ours through Christ, who loved us.

[38] And I am convinced that nothing can ever separate us from God's love. Neither death nor life, neither angels nor demons, neither our fears for today nor our worries about tomorrow—not even the powers of hell can separate us from God's love. [39] No power in the sky above or in the earth below—indeed, nothing in all creation will ever be able to separate us from the love of God that is revealed in Christ Jesus our Lord.

Romans 8:37-39 New Living Translation (NLT)

Daily Memoir

_____

_____

_____

_____

_____

_____

_____

_____

_____

_____

DAY 204

Daily Message

Unless we renew our minds on purpose to think like God we will be conformed to the way the world does things which produces failure.

Daily Manna

² Do not be conformed to this world (this age), [fashioned after and adapted to its external, superficial customs], but be transformed (changed) by the [entire] renewal of your mind [by its new ideals and its new attitude], so that you may prove [for yourselves] what is the good and acceptable and perfect will of God, even the thing which is good and acceptable and perfect [in His sight for you].

Romans 12:2 Amplified Bible (AMP)

Daily Memoir

_____
_____
_____
_____
_____
_____
_____
_____
_____
_____
_____
_____
_____

DAY 205

Daily Message

Renewing our mind is an everyday process that we must practice by meditating in the Word so that our thoughts, words and conduct reflect Christ!

Daily Manna

[2] And be not conformed to this world: but be ye transformed by the renewing of your mind, that ye may prove what is that good, and acceptable, and perfect, will of God.

Romans 12:2 King James Version (KJV)

Daily Memoir

_____
_____
_____
_____
_____
_____
_____
_____
_____
_____
_____
_____
_____
_____
_____

DAY 206

Daily Message

The only person with the power to renew your mind is you! God has given you His Word but it's up to you to apply it to your life and be transformed.

Daily Manna

Don't become so well-adjusted to your culture that you fit into it without even thinking. Instead, fix your attention on God. You'll be changed from the inside out. Readily recognize what he wants from you, and quickly respond to it. Unlike the culture around you, always dragging you down to its level of immaturity, God brings the best out of you, develops well-formed maturity in you.

Romans 12:2 The Message (MSG)

Daily Memoir

_____

_____

_____

_____

_____

_____

_____

_____

_____

_____

_____

_____

DAY 207

Daily Message

Christ did all the work needed to make us righteous but it is our responsibility to renew our minds to our right standing in Him.

Daily Manna

² And do not be conformed to this world, but be transformed by the renewing of your mind, so that you may prove what the will of God is, that which is good and acceptable and perfect.

Romans 12:2 New American Standard Bible (NASB)

Daily Memoir

_____
_____
_____
_____
_____
_____
_____
_____
_____
_____
_____
_____
_____
_____
_____
_____

DAY 208

Daily Message

Just because you believe something doesn't make it right; we must renew our minds to what God's Word says and reject all contradictions.

Daily Manna

[2] Do not conform to the pattern of this world, but be transformed by the renewing of your mind. Then you will be able to test and approve what God's will is—his good, pleasing and perfect will.

Romans 12:2 New International Version (NIV)

Daily Memoir

_____
_____
_____
_____
_____
_____
_____
_____
_____
_____
_____
_____
_____
_____
_____

DAY 209

Daily Message

The Word of God does not conform to circumstances; it is the circumstance that must conform to the Word in you. Going to an anointed church will help you to renew your mind in the Word.

Daily Manna

[2] And do not be conformed to this world, but be transformed by the renewing of your mind, that you may prove what *is* that good and acceptable and perfect will of God.

Romans 12:2 New King James Version (NKJV)

Daily Memoir

_____
_____
_____
_____
_____
_____
_____
_____
_____
_____
_____
_____
_____
_____

DAY 210

Daily Message

Until you purposely change the way you think from the world system to the Kingdom of God you will always get their results—defeat.

Daily Manna

[2] Don't copy the behavior and customs of this world, but let God transform you into a new person by changing the way you think. Then you will learn to know God's will for you, which is good and pleasing and perfect.

Romans 12:2 New Living Translation (NLT)

Daily Memoir

_____
_____
_____
_____
_____
_____
_____
_____
_____
_____
_____
_____
_____
_____
_____
_____
_____

DAY 211

Daily Message

Praise is your outward expression of your inward confidence that you are victorious in Christ! Never let the enemy steal your praise and you win!

Daily Manna

[57] But thanks be to God, Who gives us the victory [making us conquerors] through our Lord Jesus Christ.

1 Corinthians 15:57 Amplified Bible (AMP)

Daily Memoir

_____
_____
_____
_____
_____
_____
_____
_____
_____
_____
_____
_____
_____
_____
_____
_____
_____
_____

DAY 212

Daily Message

God's plan is for us to walk in sweat less victory in every aspect of our lives! Victory is yours as long as you stay in Christ!

Daily Manna

[57] But thanks be to God, which giveth us the victory through our Lord Jesus Christ.

1 Corinthians 15:57 King James Version (KJV)

Daily Memoir

_____

_____

_____

_____

_____

_____

_____

_____

_____

_____

_____

_____

_____

_____

DAY 213

Daily Message

Faith is not fighting to win but realizing you have already won through Christ. Therefore continue to rejoice in Him no matter what you see!

Daily Manna

But now in a single victorious stroke of Life, all three-sin, guilt, death—are gone, the gift of our Master, Jesus Christ. Thank God!

1 Corinthians 15:57 The Message (MSG)

Daily Memoir

_____

_____

_____

_____

_____

_____

_____

_____

_____

_____

_____

_____

_____

_____

_____

_____

_____

DAY 214

Daily Message

God has made us in His image to be inferior only to Him; that means we can't be stopped! Therefore we can boldly decree: I HAVE VICTORY IN ALL THINGS THROUGH CHRIST!!!

Daily Manna

[57] but thanks be to God, who gives us the victory through our Lord Jesus Christ.

1 Corinthians 15:57 New American Standard Bible (NASB)

Daily Memoir

_____

_____

_____

_____

_____

_____

_____

_____

_____

_____

_____

_____

_____

_____

_____

_____

DAY 215

Daily Message

Praise is an act of celebration or victory! Therefore we should be in praise mode at all times because in Christ we are victorious!

Daily Manna

[57] But thanks be to God! He gives us the victory through our Lord Jesus Christ.

1 Corinthians 15:57 New International Version (NIV)

Daily Memoir

_____
_____
_____
_____
_____
_____
_____
_____
_____
_____
_____
_____
_____
_____
_____
_____
_____
_____
_____

DAY 216

Daily Message

Failure is not an option IN CHRIST! Keep abiding in the Word and praising Him for the victory; you were created to be more than a conqueror! YOU WIN!

Daily Manna

[57] But thanks *be* to God, who gives us the victory through our Lord Jesus Christ.

1 Corinthians 15:57 New King James Version (NKJV)

Daily Memoir

_____

_____

_____

_____

_____

_____

_____

_____

_____

_____

_____

_____

_____

_____

_____

_____

DAY 217

Daily Message

We serve the ALMIGHTY GOD, who can never be defeated and as long as we remain in Him we always win . . . NO MATTER WHAT! REJOICE!!!

Daily Manna

[57] But thank God! He gives us victory over sin and death through our Lord Jesus Christ.

1 Corinthians 15:57 New Living Translation (NLT)

Daily Memoir

_____
_____
_____
_____
_____
_____
_____
_____
_____
_____
_____
_____
_____
_____
_____
_____
_____
_____

DAY 218

Daily Message

Proof that you believe God's Word is that you keep rejoicing in the face of what looks like defeat knowing that you have already won!

Daily Manna

[14] But thanks be to God, Who in Christ always leads us in triumph [as trophies of Christ's victory] and through us spreads and makes evident the fragrance of the knowledge of God everywhere,

2 Corinthians 2:14 Amplified Bible (AMP)

Daily Memoir

_____
_____
_____
_____
_____
_____
_____
_____
_____
_____
_____
_____
_____
_____
_____
_____
_____
_____

DAY 219

Daily Message

Satan brings obstacles to make you think you have lost but you have to know you already won through Christ and he is defeated! Walk in victory!

Daily Manna

[14] Now thanks be unto God, which always causeth us to triumph in Christ, and maketh manifest the savour of his knowledge by us in every place.

2 Corinthians 2:14 King James Version (KJV)

Daily Memoir

DAY 220

Daily Message

We were created to think and speak like our Daddy! Don't be moved by what you see or feel; speak the Word and watch things change! YOU ARE VICTORIOUS!

Daily Manna

[14] And I got it, thank God! In the Messiah, in Christ, God leads us from place to place in one perpetual victory parade. Through us, he brings knowledge of Christ. Everywhere we go, people breathe in the exquisite fragrance.

2 Corinthians 2:14 The Message (MSG)

Daily Memoir

_____
_____
_____
_____
_____
_____
_____
_____
_____
_____
_____
_____
_____
_____
_____

DAY 221

Daily Message

In Christ you always win; make a decision to STAY in Christ (the Word) no matter what it may look like. Victory is your birthright!

Daily Manna

[14] But thanks be to God, who always leads us in triumph in Christ, and manifests through us the sweet aroma of the knowledge of Him in every place.

2 Corinthians 2:14 New American Standard Bible (NASB)

Daily Memoir

DAY 222

Daily Message

The winning game plan is consistency in the Word! Keep abiding (continuing, dwelling, remaining and staying) in Christ, Who is the Word, and He will continually lead us in triumph.

Daily Manna

[14] But thanks be to God, who always leads us as captives in Christ's triumphal procession and uses us to spread the aroma of the knowledge of him everywhere.

2 Corinthians 2:14 New International Version (NIV)

Daily Memoir

_____

_____

_____

_____

_____

_____

_____

_____

_____

_____

_____

_____

_____

_____

_____

DAY 223

Daily Message

Christ has already made us triumphant in and through Him! Stand up overcomers! Nothing can overcome us!

Daily Manna

[14] Now thanks *be* to God who always leads us in triumph in Christ, and through us diffuses the fragrance of His knowledge in every place.

2 Corinthians 2:14 New King James Version (NKJV)

Daily Memoir

_____
_____
_____
_____
_____
_____
_____
_____
_____
_____
_____
_____
_____
_____
_____
_____
_____
_____

DAY 224

Daily Message

To give up now is to give in to defeat, but if we remain in Christ we overwhelmingly overcome ALL THINGS and live in victory over the enemy!

Daily Manna

[14] But thank God! He has made us his captives and continues to lead us along in Christ's triumphal procession. Now he uses us to spread the knowledge of Christ everywhere, like a sweet perfume.

2 Corinthians 2:14 New Living Translation (NLT)

Daily Memoir

DAY 225

Daily Message

The enemy only knows how to defeat you when you open your mouth. Don't allow what you see or feel to change what you are saying. Speak the Word only!

Daily Manna

[7] For we walk by faith [we regulate our lives and conduct ourselves by our conviction or belief respecting man's relationship to God and divine things, with trust and holy fervor; thus we walk] not by sight or appearance.

2 Corinthians 5:7 Amplified Bible (AMP)

Daily Memoir

_____
_____
_____
_____
_____
_____
_____
_____
_____
_____
_____
_____
_____
_____
_____

DAY 226

Daily Message

God ALREADY has done everything He promised but it is up to you to receive the promise through Faith (acting on the Word of God). Walk it out.

Daily Manna

[7] (For we walk by faith, not by sight:)

2 Corinthians 5:7 King James Version (KJV)

Daily Memoir

_____
_____
_____
_____
_____
_____
_____
_____
_____
_____
_____
_____
_____
_____
_____
_____
_____

DAY 227

Daily Message

We combat the negative thoughts that enter our mind by opening our mouth and speaking God's Word every time a thought comes!

Daily Manna

It's what we trust in but don't yet see that keeps us going.

2 Corinthians 5:7 The Message (MSG)

Daily Memoir

_____
_____
_____
_____
_____
_____
_____
_____
_____
_____
_____
_____
_____
_____
_____
_____
_____
_____

DAY 228

Daily Message

Christ covers us in our weaknesses when we honor Him and embrace Him as our strength! Therefore we can boldly declare 'I AM STRONG!'

Daily Manna

[7] for we walk by faith, not by sight—

2 Corinthians 5:7 New American Standard Bible (NASB)

Daily Memoir

_____

_____

_____

_____

_____

_____

_____

_____

_____

_____

_____

_____

_____

_____

_____

_____

_____

_____

DAY 229

Daily Message

In all things we believe the Word of God and cast down any thought that contradicts it by opening our mouth and speaking the Word so we will have what we say.

Daily Manna

[7] For we live by faith, not by sight.

2 Corinthians 5:7 New International Version (NIV)

Daily Memoir

_____

_____

_____

_____

_____

_____

_____

_____

_____

_____

_____

_____

_____

_____

_____

_____

_____

DAY 230

Daily Message

God doesn't want Emotional Believers (who base their faith on their feelings). He wants Word Believers (who base their faith on His Word).

Daily Manna

[7] For we walk by faith, not by sight.

2 Corinthians 5:7 New King James Version (NKJV)

Daily Memoir

_____

DAY 231

Daily Message

You have to align your words with what God says about you. Stand bold on His Word and meditate on it declaring 'I am who God's Word says I am!' then say whatever the Word is.

Daily Manna

[7] For we live by believing and not by seeing.

2 Corinthians 5:7 New Living Translation (NLT)

Daily Memoir

_____
_____
_____
_____
_____
_____
_____
_____
_____
_____
_____
_____
_____
_____
_____
_____
_____
_____

DAY 232

Daily Message

Christ redeemed us from sin and the curse so we could claim our rightful inheritance to eternal life, health and prosperity! Walk in the Blessing!

Daily Manna

[13] Christ purchased our freedom [redeeming us] from the curse (doom) of the Law [and its condemnation] by [Himself] becoming a curse for us, for it is written [in the Scriptures], Cursed is everyone who hangs on a tree (is crucified);

[14] To the end that through [their receiving] Christ Jesus, the blessing [promised] to Abraham might come upon the Gentiles, so that we through faith might [all] receive [the realization of] the promise of the [Holy] Spirit.

Galatians 3:13-14 Amplified Bible (AMP)

Daily Memoir

_____

_____

_____

_____

_____

_____

_____

_____

_____

_____

_____

DAY 233

Daily Message

Bondage ends where the blood of Christ begins. Through the blood we have been redeemed from every aspect of the curse; embrace your authority!

Daily Manna

[13] Christ hath redeemed us from the curse of the law, being made a curse for us: for it is written, Cursed is every one that hangeth on a tree:

[14] That the blessing of Abraham might come on the Gentiles through Jesus Christ; that we might receive the promise of the Spirit through faith.

Galatians 3:13-14 King James Version (KJV)

Daily Memoir

_____

_____

_____

_____

_____

_____

_____

_____

_____

_____

_____

_____

_____

_____

_____

DAY 234

Daily Message

All that God promised has already been done through Christ Jesus now all you have to do is receive the work that He did and walk in the blessing.

Daily Manna

[13-14] Christ redeemed us from that self-defeating, cursed life by absorbing it completely into himself. Do you remember the Scripture that says, "Cursed is everyone who hangs on a tree"? That is what happened when Jesus was nailed to the cross: He became a curse, and at the same time dissolved the curse. And now, because of that, the air is cleared and we can see that Abraham's blessing is present and available for non-Jews, too. We are all able to receive God's life, his Spirit, in and with us by believing—just the way Abraham received it.

Galatians 3:13-14 The Message (MSG)

Daily Memoir

_____
_____
_____
_____
_____
_____
_____
_____
_____
_____
_____

DAY 235

Daily Message

Christ redeemed us from sin to put us back in a place of holiness but we have to renew our minds through speaking the Word. I AM PURE!

Daily Manna

[13] Christ redeemed us from the curse of the Law, having become a curse for us—for it is written, "CURSED IS EVERYONE WHO HANGS ON A TREE"—[14] in order that in Christ Jesus the blessing of Abraham might come to the Gentiles, so that we would receive the promise of the Spirit through faith.

Galatians 3:13-14 New American Standard Bible (NASB)

Daily Memoir

DAY 236

Daily Message

Just as you've been redeemed from sin believe the spirit of God that is within you has redeemed you from poverty, sickness and failure! You don't have to accept that!

Daily Manna

[13] Christ redeemed us from the curse of the law by becoming a curse for us, for it is written: "Cursed is everyone who is hung on a pole." [14] He redeemed us in order that the blessing given to Abraham might come to the Gentiles through Christ Jesus, so that by faith we might receive the promise of the Spirit.

Galatians 3:13-14 New International Version (NIV)

Daily Memoir

_____
_____
_____
_____
_____
_____
_____
_____
_____
_____
_____
_____
_____

DAY 237

Daily Message

Through Jesus Christ we have the promise, that if we abide in Him and be fully persuaded in the faith we will have whatever we ask!

Daily Manna

[13] Christ has redeemed us from the curse of the law, having become a curse for us (for it is written, *"Cursed is everyone who hangs on a tree"*), [14] that the blessing of Abraham might come upon the Gentiles in Christ Jesus, that we might receive the promise of the Spirit through faith.

Galatians 3:13-14 New King James Version (NKJV)

Daily Memoir

_____

_____

_____

_____

_____

_____

_____

_____

_____

_____

_____

_____

_____

_____

_____

DAY 238

Daily Message

You are an Heir to the Promise but unless you know and believe the Word (Christ) you will forfeit your rightful inheritance. Get the Word, live Blessed!

Daily Manna

[13] But Christ has rescued us from the curse pronounced by the law. When he was hung on the cross, he took upon himself the curse for our wrongdoing. For it is written in the Scriptures, "Cursed is everyone who is hung on a tree." [14] Through Christ Jesus, God has blessed the Gentiles with the same blessing he promised to Abraham, so that we who are believers might receive the promised Holy Spirit through faith.

Galatians 3:13-14 New Living Translation (NLT)

Daily Memoir

DAY 239

Daily Message

God has already predestined you for greatness but you must change your perspective of His Word to see the Blessing manifest in your life!

Daily Manna

[10] For we are God's [own] handiwork (His workmanship), recreated in Christ Jesus, [born anew] that we may do those good works which God predestined (planned beforehand) for us [taking paths which He prepared ahead of time], that we should walk in them [living the good life which He prearranged and made ready for us to live].

Ephesians 2:10 Amplified Bible (AMP)

Daily Memoir

_____
_____
_____
_____
_____
_____
_____
_____
_____
_____
_____
_____
_____
_____
_____

DAY 240

Daily Message

We are not here to be served by God but to serve Him so that His glory will be manifested through us to fulfill His purpose!

Daily Manna

[10] For we are his workmanship, created in Christ Jesus unto good works, which God hath before ordained that we should walk in them.

Ephesians 2:10 King James Version (KJV)

Daily Memoir

_____

_____

_____

_____

_____

_____

_____

_____

_____

_____

_____

_____

_____

_____

_____

_____

_____

DAY 241

Daily Message

GOD has already predestined what path we need to take for the good life. Why not seek Him for every turn so you can stay on the path?

Daily Manna

He creates each of us by Christ Jesus to join him in the work he does, the good work he has gotten ready for us to do, work we had better be doing.

Ephesians 2:10 The Message (MSG)

Daily Memoir

_____
_____
_____
_____
_____
_____
_____
_____
_____
_____
_____
_____
_____
_____
_____
_____
_____
_____

DAY 242

Daily Message

We cannot be co-workers with God if we don't know what His vision is; make His plan your priority and you will surely walk in the good life.

Daily Manna

[10] For we are His workmanship, created in Christ Jesus for good works, which God prepared beforehand so that we would walk in them.

Ephesians 2:10 New American Standard Bible (NASB)

Daily Memoir

_____
_____
_____
_____
_____
_____
_____
_____
_____
_____
_____
_____
_____
_____
_____
_____
_____
_____
_____

DAY 243

Daily Message

Choose to be a co-healer of the Body of Christ; not a co-harmer! Power flows when we join together in His name. We need one another!

Daily Manna

[10] For we are God's handiwork, created in Christ Jesus to do good works, which God prepared in advance for us to do.

Ephesians 2:10 New International Version (NIV)

Daily Memoir

_____
_____
_____
_____
_____
_____
_____
_____
_____
_____
_____
_____
_____
_____
_____
_____
_____
_____

DAY 244

Daily Message

When you abide in the Word and surround yourself with people who will challenge you to grow up there is nothing that will stop you from manifesting God's greatness in you!

Daily Manna

[10] For we are His workmanship, created in Christ Jesus for good works, which God prepared beforehand that we should walk in them.

Ephesians 2:10 New King James Version (NKJV)

Daily Memoir

_____

_____

_____

_____

_____

_____

_____

_____

_____

_____

_____

_____

_____

_____

_____

_____

_____

DAY 245

Daily Message

God created you for a specific purpose therefore align your words with God's so that you may fulfill your purpose and walk in the good life.

Daily Manna

[10] For we are God's masterpiece. He has created us anew in Christ Jesus, so we can do the good things he planned for us long ago.

Ephesians 2:10 New Living Translation (NLT)

Daily Memoir

_____
_____
_____
_____
_____
_____
_____
_____
_____
_____
_____
_____
_____
_____
_____
_____
_____
_____

DAY 246

Daily Message

God has empowered us to change the world but first we must use that power working in us to change ourselves (the way we think) today!

Daily Manna

[20] Now to Him Who, by (in consequence of) the [action of His] power that is at work within us, is able to [carry out His purpose and] do superabundantly, far over and above all that we [dare] ask or think [infinitely beyond our highest prayers, desires, thoughts, hopes, or dreams]—

Ephesians 3:20 Amplified Bible (AMP)

Daily Memoir

_____
_____
_____
_____
_____
_____
_____
_____
_____
_____
_____
_____
_____
_____

DAY 247

Daily Message

There is nothing/no one greater than God but your victory is NOT ONLY dependent on Him, it's your trust in His power working in you.

Daily Manna

[20] Now unto him that is able to do exceeding abundantly above all that we ask or think, according to the power that worketh in us,

Ephesians 3:20 King James Version (KJV)

Daily Memoir

_____
_____
_____
_____
_____
_____
_____
_____
_____
_____
_____
_____
_____
_____
_____
_____
_____

DAY 248

Daily Message

The power of God works in us as we completely submit and obey His Word; acting on what He has said by aligning our words with His.

Daily Manna

[20] God can do anything, you know—far more than you could ever imagine or guess or request in your wildest dreams! He does it not by pushing us around but by working within us, his Spirit deeply and gently within us.

Ephesians 3:20 The Message (MSG)

Daily Memoir

_____
_____
_____
_____
_____
_____
_____
_____
_____
_____
_____
_____
_____
_____
_____
_____

DAY 249

Daily Message

Grace is God's ability to do exceedingly, abundantly more than you ask or think according to His Word working in you. Work the Word!

Daily Manna

[20] Now to Him who is able to do far more abundantly beyond all that we ask or think, according to the power that works within us,

Ephesians 3:20 New American Standard Bible (NASB)

Daily Memoir

_____
_____
_____
_____
_____
_____
_____
_____
_____
_____
_____
_____
_____
_____
_____
_____
_____

DAY 250

Daily Message

God can and will do exceedingly, above all that we think or ask when we are fully persuaded in the faith of His Word (Christ) that powerfully works in us.

Daily Manna

[20] Now to him who is able to do immeasurably more than all we ask or imagine, according to his power that is at work within us,

Ephesians 3:20 New International Version (NIV)

Daily Memoir

_____
_____
_____
_____
_____
_____
_____
_____
_____
_____
_____
_____
_____
_____

DAY 251

Daily Message

ARISE and take the limits off your mind. GOD IS ABLE to do MORE through you when you make the Word BIGGER than what you see and activate His LIMITLESS POWER IN YOU!

Daily Manna

[20] Now to Him who is able to do exceedingly abundantly above all that we ask or think, according to the power that works in us,

Ephesians 3:20 New King James Version (NKJV)

Daily Memoir

_____
_____
_____
_____
_____
_____
_____
_____
_____
_____
_____
_____
_____
_____
_____
_____
_____

DAY 252

Daily Message

God is faithful to perform everything you ask according to His Word when your heart is committed to Him. Today align your heart with His plan!

Daily Manna

[20] Now all glory to God, who is able, through his mighty power at work within us, to accomplish infinitely more than we might ask or think.

Ephesians 3:20 New Living Translation (NLT)

Daily Memoir

_____
_____
_____
_____
_____
_____
_____
_____
_____
_____
_____
_____
_____
_____
_____
_____
_____
_____

DAY 253

Daily Message

Be mindful of how you treat people; the same respect or disregard you show to them is a seed you are sowing in your own life.

Daily Manna

[1] SO BY whatever [appeal to you there is in our mutual dwelling in Christ, by whatever] strengthening and consoling and encouraging [our relationship] in Him [affords], by whatever persuasive incentive there is in love, by whatever participation in the [Holy] Spirit [we share], and by whatever depth of affection and compassionate sympathy, [2] Fill up and complete my joy by living in harmony and being of the same mind and one in purpose, having the same love, being in full accord and of one harmonious mind and intention. [3] Do nothing from factional motives [through contentiousness, strife, selfishness, or for unworthy ends] or prompted by conceit and empty arrogance. Instead, in the true spirit of humility (lowliness of mind) let each regard the others as better than and superior to himself [thinking more highly of one another than you do of yourselves]. [4] Let each of you esteem and look upon and be concerned for not [merely] his own interests, but also each for the interests of others. [5] Let this same attitude and purpose and [humble] mind be in you which was in Christ Jesus: [Let Him be your example in humility:]

Philippians 2:1-5 Amplified Bible (AMP)

Daily Memoir

DAY 254

Daily Message

Surround yourself with people who are Christ-minded so that they may challenge you to renew your mind and be set apart as God desires.

Daily Manna

[1] If there be therefore any consolation in Christ, if any comfort of love, if any fellowship of the Spirit, if any bowels and mercies, [2] Fulfil ye my joy, that ye be likeminded, having the same love, being of one accord, of one mind. [3] Let nothing be done through strife or vainglory; but in lowliness of mind let each esteem other better than themselves. [4] Look not every man on his own things, but every man also on the things of others. [5] Let this mind be in you, which was also in Christ Jesus:

Philippians 2:1-5 King James Version (KJV)

Daily Memoir

_____
_____
_____
_____
_____
_____
_____
_____
_____
_____
_____
_____
_____

DAY 255

Daily Message

As we embrace being Christ-centered and others-focused God will entrust us with more and manifest His blessings in and through us.

Daily Manna

1-5 If you've gotten anything at all out of following Christ, if his love has made any difference in your life, if being in a community of the Spirit means anything to you, if you have a heart, if you care—then do me a favor: Agree with each other, love each other, be deep-spirited friends. Don't push your way to the front; don't sweet-talk your way to the top. Put yourself aside, and help others get ahead. Don't be obsessed with getting your own advantage. Forget yourselves long enough to lend a helping hand. Think of yourselves the way Christ Jesus thought of himself.

Philippians 2:1-5 The Message (MSG)

Daily Memoir

_____

_____

_____

_____

_____

_____

_____

_____

_____

_____

_____

DAY 256

Daily Message

Love is unselfish; we must purposely abide in the love of Christ to lay aside our selfish motives and put the needs of others above our own.

Daily Manna

[1] Therefore if there is any encouragement in Christ, if there is any consolation of love, if there is any fellowship of the Spirit, if any affection and compassion, [2] make my joy complete by being of the same mind, maintaining the same love, united in spirit, intent on one purpose. [3] Do nothing from selfishness or empty conceit, but with humility of mind regard one another as more important than yourselves; [4] do not *merely* look out for your own personal interests, but also for the interests of others. [5] Have this attitude in yourselves which was also in Christ Jesus,

Philippians 2:1-5 New American Standard Bible (NASB)

Daily Memoir

_____

_____

_____

_____

_____

_____

_____

_____

_____

_____

DAY 257

Daily Message

The blessing is the anointing (empowerment/ability) you are given to be a blessing to someone else. Through unselfishly blessing others you will be blessed.

Daily Manna

[1] Therefore if you have any encouragement from being united with Christ, if any comfort from his love, if any common sharing in the Spirit, if any tenderness and compassion, [2] then make my joy complete by being like-minded, having the same love, being one in spirit and of one mind. [3] Do nothing out of selfish ambition or vain conceit. Rather, in humility value others above yourselves, [4] not looking to your own interests but each of you to the interests of the others. [5] In your relationships with one another, have the same mindset as Christ Jesus:

Philippians 2:1-5 New International Version (NIV)

Daily Memoir

_____

_____

_____

_____

_____

_____

_____

_____

_____

DAY 258

To obey God we must (on purpose) set aside our selfish motives and say yes to His perfect will so that His purpose will be fulfilled in the earth.

Daily Manna

[1] Therefore if *there is* any consolation in Christ, if any comfort of love, if any fellowship of the Spirit, if any affection and mercy, [2] fulfill my joy by being like-minded, having the same love, *being* of one accord, of one mind. [3] *Let* nothing *be done* through selfish ambition or conceit, but in lowliness of mind let each esteem others better than himself. [4] Let each of you look out not only for his own interests, but also for the interests of others. [5] Let this mind be in you which was also in Christ Jesus,

Philippians 2:1-5 New King James Version (NKJV)

Daily Memoir

_____
_____
_____
_____
_____
_____
_____
_____
_____
_____
_____

DAY 259

Daily Message

We are commanded to serve one another as we would Christ Himself, not with the motive of receiving praise from men but in obedience to God.

Daily Manna

[1] Is there any encouragement from belonging to Christ? Any comfort from his love? Any fellowship together in the Spirit? Are your hearts tender and compassionate? [2] Then make me truly happy by agreeing wholeheartedly with each other, loving one another, and working together with one mind and purpose. [3] Don't be selfish; don't try to impress others. Be humble, thinking of others as better than yourselves. [4] Don't look out only for your own interests, but take an interest in others, too. [5] You must have the same attitude that Christ Jesus had.

Philippians 2:1-5 New Living Translation (NLT)

Daily Memoir

_____
_____
_____
_____
_____
_____
_____
_____
_____
_____

DAY 260

Daily Message

Since we are assured that if we set our minds on God's Word we will have perfect peace we ought to consistently think and speak it.

Daily Manna

⁷ And God's peace [shall be yours, that tranquil state of a soul assured of its salvation through Christ, and so fearing nothing from God and being content with its earthly lot of whatever sort that is, that peace] which transcends all understanding shall garrison and mount guard over your hearts and minds in Christ Jesus.
⁸ For the rest, brethren, whatever is true, whatever is worthy of reverence and is honorable and seemly, whatever is just, whatever is pure, whatever is lovely and lovable, whatever is kind and winsome and gracious, if there is any virtue and excellence, if there is anything worthy of praise, think on and weigh and take account of these things [fix your minds on them].

Philippians 4:7-8 Amplified Bible (AMP)

Daily Memoir

_____
_____
_____
_____
_____
_____
_____
_____
_____

DAY 261

Daily Message

Whatever dominates your thoughts is what you ultimately become. Let God's Word be your dominate thought and speak it until it is manifested in you.

Daily Manna

[7] And the peace of God, which passeth all understanding, shall keep your hearts and minds through Christ Jesus.

[8] Finally, brethren, whatsoever things are true, whatsoever things are honest, whatsoever things are just, whatsoever things are pure, whatsoever things are lovely, whatsoever things are of good report; if there be any virtue, and if there be any praise, think on these things.

Philippians 4:7-8 King James Version (KJV)

Daily Memoir

DAY 262

Daily Message

God is peace and will place us in His peace in the midst of EVERYTHING if we keep our mind on Him (remain focused on His Word) at all times.

Daily Manna

[7] Before you know it, a sense of God's wholeness, everything coming together for good, will come and settle you down. It's wonderful what happens when Christ displaces worry at the center of your life.

[8] Summing it all up, friends, I'd say you'll do best by filling your minds and meditating on things true, noble, reputable, authentic, compelling, gracious—the best, not the worst; the beautiful, not the ugly; things to praise, not things to curse.

Philippians 4:8 The Message (MSG)

Daily Memoir

_____

_____

_____

_____

_____

_____

_____

_____

_____

_____

_____

DAY 263

Daily Message

In order to think about your problems you would have to take your mind off the Word (Christ) and a mind without the Word is already defeated. Think on these things.

Daily Manna

[7] And the peace of God, which surpasses all comprehension, will guard your hearts and your minds in Christ Jesus.

[8] Finally, brethren, whatever is true, whatever is honorable, whatever is right, whatever is pure, whatever is lovely, whatever is of good repute, if there is any excellence and if anything worthy of praise, dwell on these things.

Philippians 4:8 New American Standard Bible (NASB)

Daily Memoir

_____

_____

_____

_____

_____

_____

_____

_____

_____

_____

_____

_____

_____

DAY 264

Daily Message

This is the day the Lord has made don't stop rejoicing! LOOK UP; set your mind on the Word working in you to give you victory in all things!

Daily Manna

[7] And the peace of God, which transcends all understanding, will guard your hearts and your minds in Christ Jesus.

[8] Finally, brothers and sisters, whatever is true, whatever is noble, whatever is right, whatever is pure, whatever is lovely, whatever is admirable—if anything is excellent or praiseworthy—think about such things.

Philippians 4:8 New International Version (NIV)

Daily Memoir

_____

_____

_____

_____

_____

_____

_____

_____

_____

_____

_____

_____

_____

DAY 265

Daily Message

This is the day the LORD has made; a new day of mercy, grace and abundant life in Him! That's more than enough reason to rejoice!

Daily Manna

[7] and the peace of God, which surpasses all understanding, will guard your hearts and minds through Christ Jesus.

[8] Finally, brethren, whatever things are true, whatever things *are* noble, whatever things *are* just, whatever things *are* pure, whatever things *are* lovely, whatever things *are* of good report, if *there is* any virtue and if *there is* anything praiseworthy—meditate on these things.

Philippians 4:8 New King James Version (NKJV)

Daily Memoir

_____

_____

_____

_____

_____

_____

_____

_____

_____

_____

_____

_____

DAY 266

Daily Message

Stop talking about the struggle; the Word says you are MORE THAN a conqueror! Stop reliving your past, believe and speak the Word over your life!

Daily Manna

[7] Then you will experience God's peace, which exceeds anything we can understand. His peace will guard your hearts and minds as you live in Christ Jesus.

[8] And now, dear brothers and sisters, one final thing. Fix your thoughts on what is true, and honorable, and right, and pure, and lovely, and admirable. Think about things that are excellent and worthy of praise.

Philippians 4:8 New Living Translation (NLT)

Daily Memoir

_____
_____
_____
_____
_____
_____
_____
_____
_____
_____
_____
_____
_____

DAY 267

Daily Message

Until you realize you are nothing without Christ you will not accomplish anything of value for Him.

Daily Manna

[13] I have strength for all things in Christ Who empowers me [I am ready for anything and equal to anything through Him Who infuses inner strength into me; I am self-sufficient in Christ's sufficiency].

Philippians 4:13 Amplified Bible (AMP)

Daily Memoir

_____
_____
_____
_____
_____
_____
_____
_____
_____
_____
_____
_____
_____
_____
_____
_____
_____

DAY 268

Daily Message

You will never accomplish what God wants you to do trying to do it through your own strength. Those who abide in Him accomplish great things!

Daily Manna

[13] I can do all things through Christ which strengtheneth me.

Philippians 4:13 King James Version (KJV)

Daily Memoir

DAY 269

Daily Message

The key to winning is remaining IN CHRIST! It is through Him we are victorious; not by our strength alone.

Daily Manna

Whatever I have, wherever I am, I can make it through anything in the One who makes me who I am.

Philippians 4:13 The Message (MSG)

Daily Memoir

_____
_____
_____
_____
_____
_____
_____
_____
_____
_____
_____
_____
_____
_____
_____
_____
_____
_____

DAY 270

Daily Message

God can do ALL THINGS through those who remain planted in His Word!!

Daily Manna

[13] I can do all things through Him who strengthens me.

Philippians 4:13 New American Standard Bible (NASB)

Daily Memoir

_____

_____

_____

_____

_____

_____

_____

_____

_____

_____

_____

_____

_____

_____

_____

_____

_____

DAY 271

Daily Message

There is no greater power than God's love and as we abide in His love we are empowered to fulfill what we were created to do.

Daily Manna

[13] I can do all this through him who gives me strength.

Philippians 4:13 New International Version (NIV)

Daily Memoir

_____
_____
_____
_____
_____
_____
_____
_____
_____
_____
_____
_____
_____
_____
_____
_____
_____
_____

DAY 272

Daily Message

In order to move forward into the future God has for you, stop thinking and speaking about your past as if it is your today and press on!

Daily Manna

[13] I can do all things through Christ who strengthens me.

Philippians 4:13 New King James Version (NKJV)

Daily Memoir

_____
_____
_____
_____
_____
_____
_____
_____
_____
_____
_____
_____
_____
_____
_____
_____
_____
_____
_____

DAY 273

Daily Message

You greatest battle is for you (your born-again spirit) to overcome you (your flesh and human nature without God), but through abiding in Christ you (your spirit man) always wins!

Daily Manna

[13] For I can do everything through Christ, who gives me strength.

Philippians 4:13 New Living Translation (NLT)

Daily Memoir

_____
_____
_____
_____
_____
_____
_____
_____
_____
_____
_____
_____
_____
_____
_____
_____
_____
_____

DAY 274

Daily Message

To compare yourself to others is to disregard God and His wisdom that created you just as you are and called you good! Embrace your beauty in Christ!

Daily Manna

[4] For everything God has created is good, and nothing is to be thrown away or refused if it is received with thanksgiving.

1 Timothy 4:4 Amplified Bible (AMP)

Daily Memoir

_____
_____
_____
_____
_____
_____
_____
_____
_____
_____
_____
_____
_____
_____
_____
_____
_____

DAY 275

Daily Message

When God looks at you He sees Christ; through Him (continually abiding in the Word) you have been made complete so that the fullness of His glory is perfected in you.

Daily Manna

[4] For every creature of God is good, and nothing to be refused, if it be received with thanksgiving:

1 Timothy 4:4 King James Version (KJV)

Daily Memoir

_____
_____
_____
_____
_____
_____
_____
_____
_____
_____
_____
_____
_____
_____
_____
_____
_____

DAY 276

Daily Message

You will never properly love anyone else until you first embrace the love God has for you and truly love yourself just as He made you to be.

Daily Manna

[4] Everything God created is good, and to be received with thanks.

1 Timothy 4:4 The Message (MSG)

Daily Memoir

_____
_____
_____
_____
_____
_____
_____
_____
_____
_____
_____
_____
_____
_____
_____
_____
_____
_____

DAY 277

Daily Message

When we consider the works of God's hands we must stand in awe of the God who created us in His image and crowned us with His glory!

Daily Manna

[4] For everything created by God is good, and nothing is to be rejected if it is received with gratitude;

1 Timothy 4:4 New American Standard Bible (NASB)

Daily Memoir

_____
_____
_____
_____
_____
_____
_____
_____
_____
_____
_____
_____
_____
_____
_____
_____
_____

DAY 278

Daily Message

If you see no value in whom God made you to BE you will always DO things to be valued by others. God values you as the "you" He called you to be! Be You:)

Daily Manna

[4] For everything God created is good, and nothing is to be rejected if it is received with thanksgiving,

1 Timothy 4:4 New International Version (NIV)

Daily Memoir

_____

_____

_____

_____

_____

_____

_____

_____

_____

_____

_____

_____

_____

_____

_____

_____

_____

DAY 279

Daily Message

The enemy hates you because you were created in the image of God which makes you SUPERIOR over him! Don't let him make you think anything less.

Daily Manna

[4] For every creature of God *is* good, and nothing is to be refused if it is received with thanksgiving;

1 Timothy 4:4 New King James Version (NKJV)

Daily Memoir

_____

_____

_____

_____

_____

_____

_____

_____

_____

_____

_____

_____

_____

_____

_____

DAY 280

Daily Message

You are representing Christ in the earth so it is His Words that should continually fill your heart and mouth. Abide in the Word so Christ can be seen in you.

Daily Manna

[4] Since everything God created is good, we should not reject any of it but receive it with thanks.

1 Timothy 4:4 New Living Translation (NLT)

Daily Memoir

_____
_____
_____
_____
_____
_____
_____
_____
_____
_____
_____
_____
_____
_____
_____
_____

DAY 281

Daily Message

We hope in the Word until it produces faith, we hold to our faith in the Word until it produces patience and through faith and patience we receive the promise.

Daily Manna

[12] In order that you may not grow disinterested and become [spiritual] sluggards, but imitators, behaving as do those who through faith (by their leaning of the entire personality on God in Christ in absolute trust and confidence in His power, wisdom, and goodness) and by practice of patient endurance and waiting are [now] inheriting the promises.

Hebrews 6:12 Amplified Bible (AMP)

Daily Memoir

DAY 282

Daily Message

It is the Word of God that we BELIEVE and SPEAK that is manifested in and through us, CONTINUE in the Word and speak it until the manifestation happens.

Daily Manna

[12] That ye be not slothful, but followers of them who through faith and patience inherit the promises.

Hebrews 6:12 King James Version (KJV)

Daily Memoir

_____

_____

_____

_____

_____

_____

_____

_____

_____

_____

_____

_____

_____

_____

_____

_____

DAY 283

Daily Message

God's way of doing things takes faith (acting on the Word) and patience (continuing to stand on what you believe). Don't give up!

Daily Manna

[12] Don't drag your feet. Be like those who stay the course with committed faith and then get everything promised to them.

Hebrews 6:12 The Message (MSG)

Daily Memoir

_____
_____
_____
_____
_____
_____
_____
_____
_____
_____
_____
_____
_____
_____
_____
_____
_____

DAY 284

Daily Message

It is through faith and patience you receive the Promise! Therefore act on the Word and refuse to be moved from what you believe until you get it!

Daily Manna

[12] so that you will not be sluggish, but imitators of those who through faith and patience inherit the promises.

Hebrews 6:12 New American Standard Bible (NASB)

Daily Memoir

_____
_____
_____
_____
_____
_____
_____
_____
_____
_____
_____
_____
_____
_____
_____
_____
_____
_____

DAY 285

Daily Message

It's impossible for you to walk in the blessing if you don't regularly GO TO CHURCH and have a pastor who teaches you to imitate their faith by abiding in the Word of God.

Daily Manna

[12] We do not want you to become lazy, but to imitate those who through faith and patience inherit what has been promised.

Hebrews 6:12 New International Version (NIV)

Daily Memoir

_____
_____
_____
_____
_____
_____
_____
_____
_____
_____
_____
_____
_____
_____
_____
_____

DAY 286

Daily Message

We don't get the promises of God just because we want them; we have to act on the Word through imitating the faith we see in our leaders.

Daily Manna

[12] that you do not become sluggish, but imitate those who through faith and patience inherit the promises.

Hebrews 6:12 New King James Version (NKJV)

Daily Memoir

_____
_____
_____
_____
_____
_____
_____
_____
_____
_____
_____
_____
_____
_____
_____
_____
_____
_____
_____

DAY 287

Daily Message

Even if God doesn't do things when you think He should or how you think He should trust His plan more than your own understanding!

Daily Manna

[12] Then you will not become spiritually dull and indifferent. Instead, you will follow the example of those who are going to inherit God's promises because of their faith and endurance.

Hebrews 6:12 New Living Translation (NLT)

Daily Memoir

_____
_____
_____
_____
_____
_____
_____
_____
_____
_____
_____
_____
_____
_____
_____
_____

DAY 288

Daily Message

Your past does not dictate your future but what you're saying today will!
Speak to your future starting NOW.

Daily Manna

[1] NOW FAITH is the assurance (the confirmation, the title deed) of
the things [we] hope for, being the proof of things [we] do not see and the
conviction of their reality [faith perceiving as real fact what is not revealed
to the senses].

Hebrews 11:1 Amplified Bible (AMP)

Daily Memoir

_____
_____
_____
_____
_____
_____
_____
_____
_____
_____
_____
_____
_____
_____
_____
_____

DAY 289

Daily Message

Faith is an act of will that says 'I will believe God's Word no matter what!' then living your life in agreement with that.

Daily Manna

[1] Now faith is the substance of things hoped for, the evidence of things not seen.

Hebrews 11:1 King James Version (KJV)

Daily Memoir

_____
_____
_____
_____
_____
_____
_____
_____
_____
_____
_____
_____
_____
_____
_____
_____
_____

DAY 290

Daily Message

Trusting God is being committed to believing what His Word promises no matter how long it takes or what you see in the natural.

Daily Manna

[1] The fundamental fact of existence is that this trust in God, this faith, is the firm foundation under everything that makes life worth living. It's our handle on what we can't see.

Hebrews 11:1 The Message (MSG)

Daily Memoir

_____

_____

_____

_____

_____

_____

_____

_____

_____

_____

_____

_____

_____

_____

DAY 291

Daily Message

Faith is having confidence in God's Word; the ability to see pass what is seen in the natural and keep speaking and believing His Word.

Daily Manna

[1] Now faith is the assurance of *things* hoped for, the conviction of things not seen.

Hebrews 11:1 New American Standard Bible (NASB)

Daily Memoir

_____
_____
_____
_____
_____
_____
_____
_____
_____
_____
_____
_____
_____
_____
_____
_____
_____

DAY 292

Daily Message

Faith is an action word; we believe God's Word therefore we act on what we believe by speaking what God has said about the situation.

Daily Manna

[1] Now faith is confidence in what we hope for and assurance about what we do not see.

Hebrews 11:1 New International Version (NIV)

Daily Memoir

_____

_____

_____

_____

_____

_____

_____

_____

_____

_____

_____

_____

_____

_____

_____

_____

_____

DAY 293

Daily Message

Faith is not just knowing God's Word but obeying it. So aim to always please God through obedience and then make way for the blessings!

Daily Manna

[1] Now faith is the substance of things hoped for, the evidence of things not seen.

Hebrews 11:1 New King James Version (NKJV)

Daily Memoir

_____

_____

_____

_____

_____

_____

_____

_____

_____

_____

_____

_____

_____

_____

_____

_____

DAY 294

Daily Message

Once you grab hold of God's word (by implanting it in your heart) you ALREADY possess whatever you're asking for so thank God NOW until the manifestation arrives.

Daily Manna

[1] Faith is the confidence that what we hope for will actually happen; it gives us assurance about things we cannot see.

Hebrews 11:1 New Living Translation (NLT)

Daily Memoir

_____
_____
_____
_____
_____
_____
_____
_____
_____
_____
_____
_____
_____
_____
_____
_____
_____

DAY 295

Daily Message

God is not moved by the words we speak or how we feel but by His Word we speak despite what we feel. Faith is Word-based!

Daily Manna

⁶ But without faith it is impossible to please and be satisfactory to Him. For whoever would come near to God must [necessarily] believe that God exists and that He is the rewarder of those who earnestly and diligently seek Him [out].

Hebrews 11:6 Amplified Bible (AMP)

Daily Memoir

_____
_____
_____
_____
_____
_____
_____
_____
_____
_____
_____
_____
_____
_____
_____
_____

DAY 296

Daily Message

God has already done EVERYTHING He promised now you just have to stand on His Word until you see the manifestation and do not be moved.

Daily Manna

[6] But without faith it is impossible to please him: for he that cometh to God must believe that he is, and that he is a rewarder of them that diligently seek him.

Hebrews 11:6 King James Version (KJV)

Daily Memoir

_____
_____
_____
_____
_____
_____
_____
_____
_____
_____
_____
_____
_____
_____
_____
_____
_____

DAY 297

Daily Message

Refuse to be moved! God has already fulfilled His part of the Promise you just have to stand on the Word until it comes to pass!

Daily Manna

[6] It's impossible to please God apart from faith. And why? Because anyone who wants to approach God must believe both that he exists and that he cares enough to respond to those who seek him.

Hebrews 11:6 The Message (MSG)

Daily Memoir

_____
_____
_____
_____
_____
_____
_____
_____
_____
_____
_____
_____
_____
_____
_____
_____

DAY 298

Daily Message

To fulfill God's purpose in your life you must stay in faith! Don't be changed by things and people around you; remain in faith and change the World!

Daily Manna

⁶ And without faith it is impossible to please *Him*, for he who comes to God must believe that He is and *that* He is a rewarder of those who seek Him.

Hebrews 11:6 New American Standard Bible (NASB)

Daily Memoir

_____
_____
_____
_____
_____
_____
_____
_____
_____
_____
_____
_____
_____
_____
_____
_____

DAY 299

Daily Message

We cannot have faith without hope but we cannot have hope only. It is our faith (acting as though the Word is true) that pleases God.

Daily Manna

[6] And without faith it is impossible to please God, because anyone who comes to him must believe that he exists and that he rewards those who earnestly seek him.

Hebrews 11:6 New International Version (NIV)

Daily Memoir

_____
_____
_____
_____
_____
_____
_____
_____
_____
_____
_____
_____
_____
_____
_____
_____

DAY 300

Daily Message

Fear is the absence of faith; have faith in God's Word knowing He would never leave or forsake you! In Him all things are possible!

Daily Manna

⁶ But without faith *it is* impossible to please *Him*, for he who comes to God must believe that He is, and *that* He is a rewarder of those who diligently seek Him.

Hebrews 11:6 New King James Version (NKJV)

Daily Memoir

_____
_____
_____
_____
_____
_____
_____
_____
_____
_____
_____
_____
_____
_____
_____
_____
_____
_____

DAY 301

Daily Message

God will ALWAYS make good on His promise to the one who pleases Him by continuing to walk by faith and not by sight.

Daily Manna

[6] And it is impossible to please God without faith. Anyone who wants to come to him must believe that God exists and that he rewards those who sincerely seek him.

Hebrews 11:6 New Living Translation (NLT)

Daily Memoir

_____
_____
_____
_____
_____
_____
_____
_____
_____
_____
_____
_____
_____
_____
_____
_____

DAY 302

Daily Message

Examine your motives for seeking God. Is it so He will do things for you or is it so you can be closer to Him to fulfill His desires?

Daily Manna

[2] You are jealous and covet [what others have] and your desires go unfulfilled; [so] you become murderers. [To hate is to murder as far as your hearts are concerned.] You burn with envy and anger and are not able to obtain [the gratification, the contentment, and the happiness that you seek], so you fight and war. You do not have, because you do not ask. [I John 3:15.] [3] [Or] you do ask [God for them] and yet fail to receive, because you ask with wrong purpose and evil, selfish motives. Your intention is [when you get what you desire] to spend it in sensual pleasures.

James 4:2-3 Amplified Bible (AMP)

Daily Memoir

DAY 303

Daily Message

If your commitment to God is based on what He gives you then you will never receive anything from Him because your heart was never truly His from the start.

Daily Manna

[2] Ye lust, and have not: ye kill, and desire to have, and cannot obtain: ye fight and war, yet ye have not, because ye ask not. [3] Ye ask, and receive not, because ye ask amiss, that ye may consume it upon your lusts.

James 4:2-3 King James Version (KJV)

Daily Memoir

_____
_____
_____
_____
_____
_____
_____
_____
_____
_____
_____
_____
_____
_____

DAY 304

Daily Message

It is the unselfish motives of the heart that God honors. Is your prayer beneficial to others or just yourself? We ought to be Christ-centered; others-focused.

Daily Manna

[2-3] You lust for what you don't have and are willing to kill to get it. You want what isn't yours and will risk violence to get your hands on it. You wouldn't think of just asking God for it, would you? And why not? Because you know you'd be asking for what you have no right to. You're spoiled children, each wanting your own way.

James 4:2-3 The Message (MSG)

Daily Memoir

_____

_____

_____

_____

_____

_____

_____

_____

_____

_____

_____

_____

DAY 305

Daily Message

Make sure whatever you do is to honor God; not to get honor from people. Your motive will determine your reward.

Daily Manna

² You lust and do not have; *so* you commit murder. You are envious and cannot obtain; *so* you fight and quarrel. You do not have because you do not ask. ³ You ask and do not receive, because you ask with wrong motives, so that you may spend *it* on your pleasures.

James 4:2-3 New American Standard Bible (NASB)

Daily Memoir

_____
_____
_____
_____
_____
_____
_____
_____
_____
_____
_____
_____
_____
_____
_____

DAY 306

Daily Message

Stop looking for other people to bless you and start being a blessing to other people. You cannot reap what you have not sown.

Daily Manna

[2] You desire but do not have, so you kill. You covet but you cannot get what you want, so you quarrel and fight. You do not have because you do not ask God. [3] When you ask, you do not receive, because you ask with wrong motives, that you may spend what you get on your pleasures.

James 4:2-3 New International Version (NIV)

Daily Memoir

_____

_____

_____

_____

_____

_____

_____

_____

_____

_____

_____

_____

_____

_____

_____

_____

DAY 307

Daily Message

The fruit manifesting in your life is a product of the seeds you have sown. Be mindful that you are sowing what you want to reap.

Daily Manna

² You lust and do not have. You murder and covet and cannot obtain. You fight and war. Yet you do not have because you do not ask. ³ You ask and do not receive, because you ask amiss, that you may spend *it* on your pleasures.

James 4:2-3 New King James Version (NKJV)

Daily Memoir

_____

_____

_____

_____

_____

_____

_____

_____

_____

_____

_____

_____

_____

DAY 308

Daily Message

If your motive to love others is based on what they do for you then you don't understand God's love which is not self-serving or conditional.

Daily Manna

[2] You want what you don't have, so you scheme and kill to get it. You are jealous of what others have, but you can't get it, so you fight and wage war to take it away from them. Yet you don't have what you want because you don't ask God for it. [3] And even when you ask, you don't get it because your motives are all wrong—you want only what will give you pleasure.

James 4:2-3 New Living Translation (NLT)

Daily Memoir

_____
_____
_____
_____
_____
_____
_____
_____
_____
_____
_____
_____
_____
_____

DAY 309

Daily Message

Taking our own cares into our hands implies that we don't trust that God's hands are big enough to handle it. Free yourself by giving it to Him.

Daily Manna

[7] Casting the whole of your care [all your anxieties, all your worries, all your concerns, once and for all] on Him, for He cares for you affectionately and cares about you watchfully.

1 Peter 5:7 Amplified Bible (AMP)

Daily Memoir

_____
_____
_____
_____
_____
_____
_____
_____
_____
_____
_____
_____
_____
_____
_____
_____

DAY 310

Daily Message

Worry never gives the result you want; all it does is put you in bondage to that circumstance. God wants you free . . . give it to Him.

Daily Manna

[7] Casting all your care upon him; for he careth for you.

1 Peter 5:7 King James Version (KJV)

Daily Memoir

_____
_____
_____
_____
_____
_____
_____
_____
_____
_____
_____
_____
_____
_____
_____
_____
_____
_____

DAY 311

Daily Message

The most perfect thing you can do is accept Christ as your Savior and continually abide in Him so that He will perfect all things that concern you.

Daily Manna

[7] Live carefree before God; he is most careful with you.

1 Peter 5:7 The Message (MSG)

Daily Memoir

_____
_____
_____
_____
_____
_____
_____
_____
_____
_____
_____
_____
_____
_____
_____
_____
_____
_____
_____
_____

DAY 312

Daily Message

Trust God as your source and cast all your cares on Him; He will continually make sure you never lack any good thing! You won't be ashamed!

Daily Manna

[7] casting all your anxiety on Him, because He cares for you.

1 Peter 5:7 New American Standard Bible (NASB)

Daily Memoir

_____

_____

_____

_____

_____

_____

_____

_____

_____

_____

_____

_____

_____

_____

_____

_____

_____

_____

DAY 313

Daily Message

The only way to be free of worry is by making the Lord your Source and trusting Him to meet all your needs. He will not fail you!

Daily Manna

[7] Cast all your anxiety on him because he cares for you.

1 Peter 5:7 New International Version (NIV)

Daily Memoir

_____
_____
_____
_____
_____
_____
_____
_____
_____
_____
_____
_____
_____
_____
_____
_____

DAY 314

Daily Message

In whatever you do make sure you are doing it as you would for the Lord . . . if you keep your mind on Him it will take the load off of you.

Daily Manna

[7] casting all your care upon Him, for He cares for you.

1 Peter 5:7 New King James Version (NKJV)

Daily Memoir

_____
_____
_____
_____
_____
_____
_____
_____
_____
_____
_____
_____
_____
_____
_____
_____
_____
_____

DAY 315

Daily Message

When you cast your problems on Christ you must immediately grab hold of His joy and peace or you will pick your problems right back up.

Daily Manna

[7] Give all your worries and cares to God, for he cares about you.

1 Peter 5:7 New Living Translation (NLT)

Daily Memoir

_____

_____

_____

_____

_____

_____

_____

_____

_____

_____

_____

_____

_____

_____

_____

_____

_____

_____

DAY 316

Daily Message

The key to success is abiding in holiness (aligning your behavior with God's by meditating on His Word and seeing yourself as He is).

Daily Manna

[15] But as the One Who called you is holy, you yourselves also be holy in all your conduct and manner of living. [16] For it is written, You shall be holy, for I am holy.

1 Peter 1:15-16 Amplified Bible (AMP)

Daily Memoir

_____
_____
_____
_____
_____
_____
_____
_____
_____
_____
_____
_____
_____
_____
_____
_____
_____

DAY 317

Daily Message

When we embrace God as Holy we will be able to see ourselves like Him so we can walk in the power of His holiness just as He created us to.

Daily Manna

[15] But as he which hath called you is holy, so be ye holy in all manner of conversation; [16] Because it is written, Be ye holy; for I am holy.

1 Peter 1:15-16 King James Version (KJV)

Daily Memoir

_____
_____
_____
_____
_____
_____
_____
_____
_____
_____
_____
_____
_____
_____
_____
_____
_____
_____
_____

DAY 318

Daily Message

God's Word is the standard for our behavior but it is our responsibility to rise to that standard by living holy in all our conduct!

Daily Manna

[15-16] As obedient children, let yourselves be pulled into a way of life shaped by God's life, a life energetic and blazing with holiness. God said, "I am holy; you be holy."

1 Peter 1:15-16 The Message (MSG)

Daily Memoir

_____
_____
_____
_____
_____
_____
_____
_____
_____
_____
_____
_____
_____
_____
_____
_____
_____

DAY 319

Daily Message

Holiness is the minimum requirement to see God but until we acknowledge we are made in His image we will not see ourselves as He is.

Daily Manna

[15] but like the Holy One who called you, be holy yourselves also in all *your* behavior; [16] because it is written, "YOU SHALL BE HOLY, FOR I AM HOLY."

1 Peter 1:15-16 New American Standard Bible (NASB)

Daily Memoir

_____
_____
_____
_____
_____
_____
_____
_____
_____
_____
_____
_____
_____
_____
_____

DAY 320

Daily Message

Everyone has a purpose but unless we are holy (aligning our thoughts and actions completely with God's Word) we will not fulfill it!

Daily Manna

[15] But just as he who called you is holy, so be holy in all you do; [16] for it is written: "Be holy, because I am holy."

1 Peter 1:15-16 New International Version (NIV)

Daily Memoir

_____
_____
_____
_____
_____
_____
_____
_____
_____
_____
_____
_____
_____
_____
_____
_____
_____

DAY 321

Daily Message

We have been set apart by the spirit of Holiness abiding in us therefore our behavior and results should be different from those in the world!

Daily Manna

[15] but as He who called you *is* holy, you also be holy in all *your* conduct, [16] because it is written, *"Be holy, for I am holy."*

1 Peter 1:15-16 New King James Version (NKJV)

Daily Memoir

_____
_____
_____
_____
_____
_____
_____
_____
_____
_____
_____
_____
_____
_____
_____
_____
_____

DAY 322

Daily Message

Being holy is not just what you do; it's the essence of who you are! God said BE HOLY so embrace that you have been made holy through Christ!

Daily Manna

[15] But now you must be holy in everything you do, just as God who chose you is holy. [16] For the Scriptures say, "You must be holy because I am holy."

1 Peter 1:15-16 New Living Translation (NLT)

Daily Memoir

_____
_____
_____
_____
_____
_____
_____
_____
_____
_____
_____
_____
_____
_____
_____
_____

DAY 323

Daily Message

The love of God leads us to use our financial goods to meet the needs of those suffering; not just spending it on our own desires.

Daily Manna

[16] By this we come to know (progressively to recognize, to perceive, to understand) the [essential] love: that He laid down His [own] life for us; and we ought to lay [our] lives down for [those who are our] brothers [in Him].

[17] But if anyone has this world's goods (resources for sustaining life) and sees his brother and fellow believer in need, yet closes his heart of compassion against him, how can the love of God live and remain in him?

1 John 3:16-17 Amplified Bible (AMP)

Daily Memoir

_____

_____

_____

_____

_____

_____

_____

_____

_____

_____

_____

_____

DAY 324

Daily Message

God's love is to see others needs as more important than our own. He didn't bless us simply for our own benefit but to be a blessing.

Daily Manna

[16] Hereby perceive we the love of God, because he laid down his life for us: and we ought to lay down our lives for the brethren.
[17] But whoso hath this world's good, and seeth his brother have need, and shutteth up his bowels of compassion from him, how dwelleth the love of God in him?

1 John 3:16-17 King James Version (KJV)

Daily Memoir

_____
_____
_____
_____
_____
_____
_____
_____
_____
_____
_____
_____
_____
_____

DAY 325

Daily Message

You were made in the God-class to be just like Him, embrace that you are made just like Love and give that love back to Him by loving His people!

Daily Manna

[16-17] This is how we've come to understand and experience love: Christ sacrificed his life for us. This is why we ought to live sacrificially for our fellow believers, and not just be out for ourselves. If you see some brother or sister in need and have the means to do something about it but turn a cold shoulder and do nothing, what happens to God's love? It disappears. And you made it disappear.

1 John 3:16-17 The Message (MSG)

Daily Memoir

DAY 326

Daily Message

Love is the root of power. For God so LOVED He has redeemed us from selfishness to place us in His love so that we may show the world His power through our Love!

Daily Manna

[16] We know love by this, that He laid down His life for us; and we ought to lay down our lives for the brethren. [17] But whoever has the world's goods, and sees his brother in need and closes his heart against him, how does the love of God abide in him?

1 John 3:16-17 New American Standard Bible (NASB)

Daily Memoir

_____
_____
_____
_____
_____
_____
_____
_____
_____
_____
_____
_____
_____
_____

DAY 327

Daily Message

You weren't saved just so you could go to heaven but so that you would be empowered to walk in your purpose and help save others so they can do the same.

Daily Manna

[16] This is how we know what love is: Jesus Christ laid down his life for us. And we ought to lay down our lives for our brothers and sisters. [17] If anyone has material possessions and sees a brother or sister in need but has no pity on them, how can the love of God be in that person?

1 John 3:16-17 New International Version (NIV)

Daily Memoir

_____
_____
_____
_____
_____
_____
_____
_____
_____
_____
_____
_____
_____
_____
_____

DAY 328

Daily Message

To love God is to love your brother through deeds not just words. God so loved that He gave and as sons of God we are commanded to do the same.

Daily Manna

[16] By this we know love, because He laid down His life for us. And we also ought to lay down *our* lives for the brethren. [17] But whoever has this world's goods, and sees his brother in need, and shuts up his heart from him, how does the love of God abide in him?

1 John 3:16-17 New King James Version (NKJV)

Daily Memoir

_____
_____
_____
_____
_____
_____
_____
_____
_____
_____
_____
_____
_____
_____
_____
_____

DAY 329

Daily Message

It is through walking in the love of God that we are empowered to forgive so that we see God's glory manifested in and through us.

Daily Manna

[16] We know what real love is because Jesus gave up his life for us. So we also ought to give up our lives for our brothers and sisters. [17] If someone has enough money to live well and sees a brother or sister in need but shows no compassion—how can God's love be in that person?

1 John 3:16-17 New Living Translation (NLT)

Daily Memoir

_____
_____
_____
_____
_____
_____
_____
_____
_____
_____
_____
_____
_____
_____
_____

DAY 330

Daily Message

There is nothing Satan can do to defeat you when you know that Christ lives in you. He has made you more than a conquer so walk in your authority!

Daily Manna

[4] Little children, you are of God [you belong to Him] and have [already] defeated and overcome them [the agents of the antichrist], because He Who lives in you is greater (mightier) than he who is in the world.

1 John 4:4 Amplified Bible (AMP)

Daily Memoir

_____
_____
_____
_____
_____
_____
_____
_____
_____
_____
_____
_____
_____
_____
_____
_____
_____

DAY 331

Daily Message

In order to overcome any obstacle you have to see yourself bigger than it; the GREATER (stronger and preeminent) ONE lives in you so YOU WIN!

Daily Manna

[4] Ye are of God, little children, and have overcome them: because greater is he that is in you, than he that is in the world.

1 John 4:4 King James Version (KJV)

Daily Memoir

_____

_____

_____

_____

_____

_____

_____

_____

_____

_____

_____

_____

_____

_____

_____

_____

_____

DAY 332

Daily Message

We serve the Almighty God but until you see Him as Great in your life you will always be defeated by the enemy. Renew your mind to His Greatness!

Daily Manna

[4] My dear children, you come from God and belong to God. You have already won a big victory over those false teachers, for the Spirit in you is far stronger than anything in the world.

1 John 4:4 The Message (MSG)

Daily Memoir

_____

_____

_____

_____

_____

_____

_____

_____

_____

_____

_____

_____

_____

_____

_____

DAY 333

Daily Message

We have been created in the image of God Almighty! In order for us to see the greatness in ourselves we must first see Him as the Great God!

Daily Manna

[4] You are from God, little children, and have overcome them; because greater is He who is in you than he who is in the world.

1 John 4:4 New American Standard Bible (NASB)

Daily Memoir

DAY 334

Daily Message

God is ALMIGHTY (no one or nothing is mightier than He) and since He is for us, living in us, there is nothing that can overcome us!

Daily Manna

[4] You, dear children, are from God and have overcome them, because the one who is in you is greater than the one who is in the world.

1 John 4:4 New International Version (NIV)

Daily Memoir

_____
_____
_____
_____
_____
_____
_____
_____
_____
_____
_____
_____
_____
_____
_____
_____
_____
_____

DAY 335

Daily Message

Life is not hard in Christ! It will take effort on your part but you are assured the sweat less victory as long as you remain in His Word!

Daily Manna

[4] You are of God, little children, and have overcome them, because He who is in you is greater than he who is in the world.

1 John 4:4 New King James Version (NKJV)

Daily Memoir

_____
_____
_____
_____
_____
_____
_____
_____
_____
_____
_____
_____
_____
_____
_____
_____
_____

DAY 336

Daily Message

Whatever you meditate on will become greater in your sight. Meditate on the Word of God, not the problem. Make the Word GREATER in you.

Daily Manna

[4] But you belong to God, my dear children. You have already won a victory over those people, because the Spirit who lives in you is greater than the spirit who lives in the world.

1 John 4:4 New Living Translation (NLT)

Daily Memoir

_____
_____
_____
_____
_____
_____
_____
_____
_____
_____
_____
_____
_____
_____
_____
_____

DAY 337

Daily Message

Since we are created in God's image the love of God in us ought to show in how we treat others. Show someone what "I love you" really means.

Daily Manna

[16] And we know (understand, recognize, are conscious of, by observation and by experience) and believe (adhere to and put faith in and rely on) the love God cherishes for us. God is love, and he who dwells and continues in love dwells and continues in God, and God dwells and continues in him. [17] In this [union and communion with Him] love is brought to completion and attains perfection with us, that we may have confidence for the day of judgment [with assurance and boldness to face Him], because as He is, so are we in this world. [18] There is no fear in love [dread does not exist], but full-grown (complete, perfect) love turns fear out of doors and expels every trace of terror! For fear brings with it the thought of punishment, and [so] he who is afraid has not reached the full maturity of love [is not yet grown into love's complete perfection].

1 John 4:16-18 Amplified Bible (AMP)

Daily Memoir

_____

_____

_____

_____

_____

_____

_____

DAY 338

Daily Message

We are the sons of God (love) so we ought to be rooted in the Word (love) and purposely walk in unconditional love with everyone just as Christ (love) does. It's all about LOVE.

Daily Manna

[16] And we have known and believed the love that God hath to us. God is love; and he that dwelleth in love dwelleth in God, and God in him. [17]Herein is our love made perfect, that we may have boldness in the day of judgment: because as he is, so are we in this world. [18]There is no fear in love; but perfect love casteth out fear: because fear hath torment. He that feareth is not made perfect in love.

1 John 4:16-18 King James Version (KJV)

Daily Memoir

_____

_____

_____

_____

_____

_____

_____

_____

_____

_____

_____

_____

DAY 339

Daily Message

We are made in the image of God, who is Love, to be love so that we may manifest His love to this unlovely world.

Daily Manna

[16-18] We know it so well, we've embraced it heart and soul, this love that comes from God. God is love. When we take up permanent residence in a life of love, we live in God and God lives in us. This way, love has the run of the house, becomes at home and mature in us, so that we're free of worry on Judgment Day—our standing in the world is identical with Christ's. There is no room in love for fear. Well-formed love banishes fear. Since fear is crippling, a fearful life—fear of death, fear of judgment—is one not yet fully formed in love.

1 John 4:16-18 The Message (MSG)

Daily Memoir

_____

_____

_____

_____

_____

_____

_____

_____

_____

_____

_____

DAY 340

Daily Message

When we know and BELIEVE God loves us and abide in His love for us nothing is impossible! GLORY TO GOD!

Daily Manna

[16] We have come to know and have believed the love which God has for us. God is love, and the one who abides in love abides in God, and God abides in him. [17] By this, love is perfected with us, so that we may have confidence in the day of judgment; because as He is, so also are we in this world. [18] There is no fear in love; but perfect love casts out fear, because fear involves punishment, and the one who fears is not perfected in love.

1 John 4:16-18 New American Standard Bible (NASB)

Daily Memoir

_____
_____
_____
_____
_____
_____
_____
_____
_____
_____
_____
_____
_____

DAY 341

Daily Message

Our connection to God is tied into our love walk with others. Just as God's love is the root of forgiveness so should our love be to others. Forgive.

Daily Manna

[16] And so we know and rely on the love God has for us. God is love. Whoever lives in love lives in God, and God in them. [17] This is how love is made complete among us so that we will have confidence on the day of judgment: In this world we are like Jesus. [18] There is no fear in love. But perfect love drives out fear, because fear has to do with punishment. The one who fears is not made perfect in love.

1 John 4:16-18 New International Version (NIV)

Daily Memoir

_____
_____
_____
_____
_____
_____
_____
_____
_____
_____
_____
_____
_____

DAY 342

Daily Message

Love and fear cannot occupy the same place; one will paralyze and cast the other out. Meditate on God's perfect love until fear flees.

Daily Manna

[16] And we have known and believed the love that God has for us. God is love, and he who abides in love abides in God, and God in him. [17] Love has been perfected among us in this: that we may have boldness in the day of judgment; because as He is, so are we in this world. [18] There is no fear in love; but perfect love casts out fear, because fear involves torment. But he who fears has not been made perfect in love.

1 John 4:16-18 New King James Version (NKJV)

Daily Memoir

_____

_____

_____

_____

_____

_____

_____

_____

_____

_____

_____

_____

DAY 343

Daily Message

Since we have been created in the image of God we ought to grow and abound in love daily because through Love we can do anything.

Daily Manna

[16] We know how much God loves us, and we have put our trust in his love. God is love, and all who live in love live in God, and God lives in them. [17] And as we live in God, our love grows more perfect. So we will not be afraid on the day of judgment, but we can face him with confidence because we live like Jesus here in this world. [18] Such love has no fear, because perfect love expels all fear. If we are afraid, it is for fear of punishment, and this shows that we have not fully experienced his perfect love.

1 John 4:16-18 New Living Translation (NLT)

Daily Memoir

_____
_____
_____
_____
_____
_____
_____
_____
_____
_____
_____

DAY 344

Daily Message

Don't let the enemy steal your confidence that God will keep His Promise! It's through your obedience to His Word that you have what you ask!

Daily Manna

[14] And this is the confidence (the assurance, the privilege of boldness) which we have in Him: [we are sure] that if we ask anything (make any request) according to His will (in agreement with His own plan), He listens to and hears us. [15]And if (since) we [positively] know that He listens to us in whatever we ask, we also know [with settled and absolute knowledge] that we have [granted us as our present possessions] the requests made of Him.

1 John 5:14-15 Amplified Bible (AMP)

Daily Memoir

_____
_____
_____
_____
_____
_____
_____
_____
_____
_____
_____
_____
_____

DAY 345

Daily Message

If you're not expecting God to do the thing you asked for there is no use in asking. You must be confident that it's already done when you ask!

Daily Manna

[14] And this is the confidence that we have in him, that, if we ask any thing according to his will, he heareth us: [15]And if we know that he hear us, whatsoever we ask, we know that we have the petitions that we desired of him.

1 John 5:14-15 King James Version (KJV)

Daily Memoir

_____

_____

_____

_____

_____

_____

_____

_____

_____

_____

_____

_____

_____

DAY 346

Daily Message

When we meditate in the Word and pray in the Spirit we build up our faith so that when we ask we are confident that we have received!

Daily Manna

[14-15] And how bold and free we then become in his presence, freely asking according to his will, sure that he's listening. And if we're confident that he's listening, we know that what we've asked for is as good as ours.

1 John 5:14-15 The Message (MSG)

Daily Memoir

_____
_____
_____
_____
_____
_____
_____
_____
_____
_____
_____
_____
_____
_____
_____
_____

DAY 347

Daily Message

We have a right to ask anything of God and be confident that we have received whatever we ask IF we continually abide in His Word.

Daily Manna

[14] This is the confidence which we have before Him, that, if we ask anything according to His will, He hears us. [15] And if we know that He hears us *in* whatever we ask, we know that we have the requests which we have asked from Him.

1 John 5:14-15 New American Standard Bible (NASB)

Daily Memoir

_____
_____
_____
_____
_____
_____
_____
_____
_____
_____
_____
_____
_____
_____
_____
_____

DAY 348

Daily Message

When we abide in the Word of God we can be confident that He hears us therefore be fully persuaded that whatever we ask we have in Jesus' name.

Daily Manna

[14] This is the confidence we have in approaching God: that if we ask anything according to his will, he hears us. [15] And if we know that he hears us—whatever we ask—we know that we have what we asked of him.

1 John 5:14-15 New International Version (NIV)

Daily Memoir

_____
_____
_____
_____
_____
_____
_____
_____
_____
_____
_____
_____
_____
_____
_____

DAY 349

Daily Message

Be confident in God and His Word that He will never forsake you (His righteousness) therefore you are blessed with more than enough to be a blessing!

Daily Manna

[14] Now this is the confidence that we have in Him, that if we ask anything according to His will, He hears us. [15] And if we know that He hears us, whatever we ask, we know that we have the petitions that we have asked of Him.

1 John 5:14-15 New King James Version (NKJV)

Daily Memoir

_____
_____
_____
_____
_____
_____
_____
_____
_____
_____
_____
_____
_____

DAY 350

Daily Message

When your confidence is complete in the Blood of Christ and His Word success is inevitable! The sight of failure is just premature success!

Daily Manna

[14] And we are confident that he hears us whenever we ask for anything that pleases him. [15] And since we know he hears us when we make our requests, we also know that he will give us what we ask for.

1 John 5:14-15 New Living Translation (NLT)

Daily Memoir

_____
_____
_____
_____
_____
_____
_____
_____
_____
_____
_____
_____
_____
_____
_____
_____

DAY 351

Daily Message

To know God is to worship Him for Who He is not just for what you want Him to do. He is God and besides Him there is no other worthy of your praise!

Daily Manna

[11] Worthy are You, our Lord and God, to receive the glory and the honor and dominion, for You created all things; by Your will they were [brought into being] and were created.

Revelation 4:11 Amplified Bible (AMP)

Daily Memoir

_____
_____
_____
_____
_____
_____
_____
_____
_____
_____
_____
_____
_____
_____

DAY 352

Daily Message

God has so divinely planned for your success that He created everything to yield to your words when you speak like Him! Only believe and speak!

Daily Manna

[11] Thou art worthy, O Lord, to receive glory and honour and power: for thou hast created all things, and for thy pleasure they are and were created.

Revelation 4:11 King James Version (KJV)

Daily Memoir

_____

_____

_____

_____

_____

_____

_____

_____

_____

_____

_____

_____

_____

_____

_____

_____

_____

_____

DAY 353

Daily Message

Anyone can praise God but only those who understand who He truly is in their lives can worship Him! Acknowledge who He is today!

Daily Manna

[11] Worthy, O Master! Yes, our God! Take the glory! the honor! the power! You created it all; It was created because you wanted it.

Revelation 4:11 The Message (MSG)

Daily Memoir

_____
_____
_____
_____
_____
_____
_____
_____
_____
_____
_____
_____
_____
_____
_____
_____
_____
_____
_____

DAY 354

Daily Message

Thanksgiving releases increase! I'm not talking about a holiday but our continual thanks to God for Who He is!

Daily Manna

[11] "Worthy are You, our Lord and our God, to receive glory and honor and power; for You created all things, and because of Your will they existed, and were created."

Revelation 4:11 New American Standard Bible (NASB)

Daily Memoir

_____
_____
_____
_____
_____
_____
_____
_____
_____
_____
_____
_____
_____
_____
_____
_____

DAY 355

Daily Message

Thank God, not just on a specific day, but every day because of who He is in your life! Give thanks for what He's done and what He's doing!

Daily Manna

[11] "You are worthy, our Lord and God, to receive glory and honor and power, for you created all things, and by your will they were created and have their being."

Revelation 4:11 New International Version (NIV)

Daily Memoir

_____
_____
_____
_____
_____
_____
_____
_____
_____
_____
_____
_____
_____
_____
_____
_____
_____

DAY 356

Daily Message

God never gave up on you; in the midst of your mess He called you good and saw fit to pull you out! That's reason enough to be thankful!

Daily Manna

[11] "You are worthy, O Lord, To receive glory and honor and power; For You created all things, And by Your will they exist and were created."

Revelation 4:11 New King James Version (NKJV)

Daily Memoir

_____
_____
_____
_____
_____
_____
_____
_____
_____
_____
_____
_____
_____
_____
_____
_____
_____
_____
_____

DAY 357

Daily Message

Confess: I am thankful that by God's grace I am what I am so I'm empowered to do what He created me for!

Daily Manna

[11] "You are worthy, O Lord our God, to receive glory and honor and power. For you created all things, and they exist because you created what you pleased."

Revelation 4:11 New Living Translation (NLT)

Daily Memoir

DAY 358

Daily Message

Since you have been redeemed by the Blood of Christ there is NOTHING that can overtake you (poverty, sickness, depression, etc.)! Just believe and speak it!

Daily Manna

[11] And they have overcome (conquered) him by means of the blood of the Lamb and by the utterance of their testimony, for they did not love and cling to life even when faced with death [holding their lives cheap till they had to die for their witnessing].

Revelation 12:11 Amplified Bible (AMP)

Daily Memoir

_____
_____
_____
_____
_____
_____
_____
_____
_____
_____
_____
_____
_____
_____

DAY 359

Daily Message

Trusting God's Word is only possible when we first trust in the Blood of Christ; which has redeemed us so we can believe in His Word.

Daily Manna

[11] And they overcame him by the blood of the Lamb, and by the word of their testimony; and they loved not their lives unto the death.

Revelation 12:11 King James Version (KJV)

Daily Memoir

_____
_____
_____
_____
_____
_____
_____
_____
_____
_____
_____
_____
_____
_____
_____
_____
_____
_____
_____

DAY 360

Daily Message

You cannot overcome until you speak like an over comer! Consistently speaking God's Word, in the face of adversity, is the key to victory!

Daily Manna

They defeated him through the blood of the Lamb and the bold word of their witness. They weren't in love with themselves; they were willing to die for Christ.

Revelation 12:11 The Message (MSG)

Daily Memoir

_____

_____

_____

_____

_____

_____

_____

_____

_____

_____

_____

_____

_____

_____

DAY 361

Daily Message

The Blood gives you full access to wealth, health, joy, peace and eternal life but it's up to you to believe and receive it!

Daily Manna

[11] And they overcame him because of the blood of the Lamb and because of the word of their testimony, and they did not love their life even when faced with death.

Revelation 12:11 New American Standard Bible (NASB)

Daily Memoir

_____
_____
_____
_____
_____
_____
_____
_____
_____
_____
_____
_____
_____
_____
_____
_____

DAY 362

Daily Message

The same Blood that freed you from sin has also freed you from sickness, poverty, lack, defeat . . . etc.! Embrace your Blood-bought right!

Daily Manna

[11] They triumphed over him by the blood of the Lamb and by the word of their testimony; they did not love their lives so much as to shrink from death.

Revelation 12:11 New International Version (NIV)

Daily Memoir

_____
_____
_____
_____
_____
_____
_____
_____
_____
_____
_____
_____
_____
_____
_____
_____
_____
_____

DAY 363

Daily Message

You are who the Word says you are so be fully persuaded that you are freed you from all things!

Daily Manna

[11] And they overcame him by the blood of the Lamb and by the word of their testimony, and they did not love their lives to the death.

Revelation 12:11 New King James Version (NKJV)

Daily Memoir

_____
_____
_____
_____
_____
_____
_____
_____
_____
_____
_____
_____
_____
_____
_____
_____
_____
_____

DAY 364

Daily Message

Through the Blood and the name of Jesus Christ we have been given all power and authority to do the impossible! The Word is power—SPEAK IT!

Daily Manna

[11] And they have defeated him by the blood of the Lamb and by their testimony. And they did not love their lives so much that they were afraid to die.

Revelation 12:11 New Living Translation (NLT)

Daily Memoir

_____

_____

_____

_____

_____

_____

_____

_____

_____

_____

_____

_____

_____

_____

_____

_____

DAY 365

Daily Message

God's not looking for New Year's resolutions! He wants committed hearts that will not be afraid and will not be moved from His Word no matter what! Fear not God is on your side so stay planted!

Daily Manna

He only is my rock and my salvation; he is my defense; I shall not be greatly moved.

Psalm 62:2 King James Version (KJV)

Daily Memoir

_____
_____
_____
_____
_____
_____
_____
_____
_____
_____
_____
_____
_____
_____
_____
_____

DAY 366

Daily Message

In order to get more from God you have to be willing to give more to Him! Give more of yourself as a living sacrifice! What are you going to give more of this year?

Daily Manna

And so, dear brothers and sisters, I plead with you to give your bodies to God because of all he has done for you. Let them be a living and holy sacrifice—the kind he will find acceptable. This is truly the way to worship him.

Romans 12:1 New Living Translation (NLT)

Daily Memoir

_____
_____
_____
_____
_____
_____
_____
_____
_____
_____
_____
_____
_____